BECOME A CERTIFIED
PERSONAL
TRAINER

Surefire Strategies to:
> Pass the Major Certification Exams
> Build a Strong Client List
> Start Making Money

ROBERT WOLFF, Ph.D.

McGraw Hill

New York Chicago San Francisco Lisbon London Madrid Mexico City
Milan New Delhi San Juan Seoul Singapore Sydney Toronto

The **McGraw·Hill** *Companies*

1 2 3 4 5 6 7 8 9 0   DOC/DOC   0 1 0 9

ISBN   978-0-07-163587-5
MHID   0-07-163587-4

McGraw-Hill books are available at special quantity discounts to use as premiums and sales promotions, or for use in corporate training programs. To contact a representative please e-mail us at bulksales@mcgraw-hill.com.

This book is printed on acid-free paper.

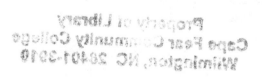

This book is dedicated to my friends Joe and Ben Weider, who devoted their lives to teaching the world the life-changing power of exercise and fitness. Thank you.

Contents

Acknowledgments

Many thanks to all those who made this book possible, including

Ron Martirano and McGraw-Hill

Dr. Sal Arria and the ISSA

Richard Cotton, Kerry O'Rourke, and the ACSM

Dr. Cedric Bryant, Todd Galati, and ACE

Paul Garbarino and the NCSF

Peter Melanson and the NSCA

Bill Staples and the NASM

Ron Clark and the NFPT

Dr. Jim Bell and the IFPA

Introduction

Those Greeks really knew their stuff—especially when it came to what the perfect human body should look like and how it should perform. The Greeks revered the human body, and those athletes who had great ones were adored for the living god–like image they displayed.

And so were those who had the "secret knowledge" of how to train them: the top trainers of their day.

Throughout history, the beauty, aesthetics, and symmetrical lines and function of the body have powerfully influenced the greatest artists, poets, sculptors, philosophers, and writers, who themselves would influence history and thought.

Just look at the magazines on the newsstands today that feature bodies and celebrities in nonstop fashion and you'll see just how little has changed.

But it's the Greeks who were really on to something, a concept so powerful that it influences the way we look at and train our bodies even today. More than 2,000 years ago, the Greeks had a vision of what the ideal body looked like and how it should perform. The Greeks marveled at the power, ability, and musculature of the physiques of warriors, wrestlers, discus throwers, runners, boxers, and other humans who possessed similar physical prowess.

They admired perfect proportion, symmetry, and beautiful body lines where one muscle flowed seamlessly into the next just like a work of art. And when the rarest of those amazing physical specimens moved into action, it truly was poetry in motion. Back in that age, the great thinkers and philosophers believed that life was about movement, and that the more movement one had, the more life and all its benefits one would experience.

Just look at how we have developed and followed our modern ways of training the body over the last 100 years or so, and it's clear just how closely our actions mirror those ancient teachings. Along with each new generation comes a new lexicon and vocabulary. Yet one of the core teachings of how we eat and how we exercise has its origins in the Greeks.

It's a philosophy called "the middle way."

The much-admired philosopher Aristotle is often the one who is credited with espousing this idea of the middle way or the "golden mean."

Its idea is simple: *In one's life, the wisest course to take is always the middle ground between too much and too little.*

Too little or too much exercise is not wise. Just the right amount of exercise is.

Too much or too little food is not wise. Just the right amount of food is.

And once you found that middle ground, the rewards of doing so were abundant.

A life of balance, harmony, proportion, reward, and virtue would be yours to enjoy, as would a long, happy, and healthy life for all your days.

A personal trainer can give his clients many of the same rewards today.

But before you become one, there's a big decision you've got to make: where and from whom are you going to get your certification credentials?

There are a lot of choices out there. So how do you know which one is best for you?

This book is going to make that decision easier.

We're going to look at the biggest, best, and most popular fitness certification organizations and let them tell you about themselves: who they are, what they do, what they offer, and how they can help you.

You are going to see sample test questions (with answers) from them, so that you'll get a good idea of what you can expect if you choose each organization and the test you'll need to pass before it will certify you.

While each organization approaches certification in different ways—and with an emphasis on different core principles compared to the others—you're going to get a good idea of the different organizations' philosophies and approaches while getting a good feel for which one of them is right for you.

I'm also going to give you a little bonus. I'll be sharing some time-tested training and success principles and strategies that people all over the world have used with great success.

After all, when it comes to your certified fitness training goals and career, there's one thing that all the organizations and I agree upon: we want you to be a great success!

The Top Certifying Organizations—Who They Are and How to Choose the Right One for You

You have a lot of choices when it comes to getting certified. Just do a Google search for "become a personal trainer" and watch how many names and Web sites pop up.

So I'm going to make it easier for you.

I'm going to give you the information on the top ones—the ones that are the most popular, have been around for years, have excellent reputations, and have solid track records for producing certified personal trainers who graduate with the skills and knowledge to produce results for the widest variety of people and applications.

Okay, so you might think just featuring these organizations and their information would be all you would need to make a good choice on which one might be best for you. And with the materials these organizations have so kindly provided for the book, you'd go a long way toward being right.

Yet, there's another factor you should pay attention to, and that's how each organization views its accreditation credentials. They aren't all the same.

In the book, you'll see that many of the organizations are accredited by the National Commission for Certifying Agencies (NCCA). Others, like the ISSA, choose Distance Education and Training Council (DETC) accreditation and will tell you their reasons for doing so.

Unlike other professions (medicine, real estate, finance, and so on), the personal training business is largely an unregulated industry that doesn't have one industrywide and generally accepted accrediting body.

That's one of the reasons why you see so many personal training certification businesses out there.

Essentially, anyone can start their own certification organization, give it a fancy name and a slick-looking Web site, take your money, send you some testing materials, and, if you pass its test, send you an official-looking piece of paper that says that you're a personal trainer.

While there may still be a bit of the Wild West out there on this unregulated prairie of personal trainer certification, look for things to move in a more regulated direction as states decide on a universal type of accreditation. Specifically, there is legislation on the horizon that seeks to develop a set of standards and benchmarks that *all* personal trainer certification organizations must follow in order for their trainers to be recognized as having the credentials and education required for someone to be called a Certified Personal Trainer.

With that in mind, before writing this book, I contacted the top certifying organizations myself. I had some specific requests for information and answers that I believed you would like to know. I want to give you the information that can help you make an informed decision on which of the certifying organizations may be right for you.

To each organization, I presented the following:

One of the central themes of the book will be to give readers (and prospective clients) a thorough overview of what the top personal trainer certification organizations are about. It's what you would like readers all over the world to know about your organization. This will include its unique approach and the philosophy behind its programs, what subject matter is included in those programs, and the reasons why it believes its approach is the most comprehensive and best available.

To help readers compare "apples to apples" so to speak, the book will feature sample test questions (with answers) for the topic areas that are featured on that organization's certification test. This will give readers a good feel for what they can expect as they decide and prepare, and allow them to see which of the top organizations may be best for them.

In the book, I would like to include from each organization at least 10 sample test questions (with answers) for every area covered in its Certified Trainer Test.

These areas will include (but are not limited to):

- The basics of human behavior and psychology
- The basics of human movement
- The basics of training assessment, testing, and workout design
- The basics of nutrition and supplementation
- The basics of safety, rehab, and injury prevention
- The basics of personal and professional success
- Other areas of interest

In addition to the above, each featured personal trainer certification organization will be highlighted further, as the book will tell readers about the history, philosophy, and practices of that organization, the certification programs and services it offers, as well as complete contact information on how readers may get in touch with that organization.

What follows in the pages of this book is the response that each certifying organization provided, accompanied by supporting material, along with my personal tools and tips for training success.

PART 1

So You Want to Become a Certified Personal Trainer

In the first half of this book, we'll cover the following:

- The top certifying organizations, their training philosophies, and the benefits their programs offer
- Test-taking options, enrollment criteria, and everything you need in order to get signed up and ready to go
- Questions, answers, and sample responses from each organization's certification exam

CHAPTER **1**

The American College of Sports Medicine

The American College of Sports Medicine (ACSM) was founded in 1954. Working in a wide range of medical specialties, allied health professions, and scientific disciplines, ACSM members are committed to the diagnosis, treatment, and prevention of sports-related injuries and the advancement of the science of exercise.

The ACSM is the largest, most respected sports medicine and exercise science organization in the world. For everyone from astronauts and athletes to people with chronic diseases or physical challenges, the ACSM continues to look for and find better methods to allow individuals to live longer and more productive lives. Healthy people make a healthier society.

Tell Me about the ACSM

Going beyond its slogan, "Advancing health through science, education, and medicine," the American College of Sports Medicine puts into practice its strategic efforts to advance the health of all. The ACSM has more than 20,000 international, national, and regional chapter members.

The ACSM's mission statement reflects its goal: "The American College of Sports Medicine promotes and integrates scientific research, education, and practical applications of sports medicine and exercise science to maintain and enhance physical performance, fitness, health, and quality of life."

ACSM's certifications cover the continuum of care, with two preventative certifications and two clinical certifications:

- *ACSM Certified Personal Trainer (CPT)*, for fitness professionals working with healthy individuals
- *ACSM Certified Health Fitness Specialist (CHFS)*, a more advanced personal trainer certification that enables fitness professionals to work with clients with medically controlled diseases
- *ACSM Certified Clinical Exercise Specialist (CCES)*, for professionals working with clients with cardiovascular, pulmonary, or metabolic diseases
- *ACSM Registered Clinical Exercise Physiologist (RCEP)*, for those working with patients with a broad spectrum of chronic diseases or disabilities

In addition, the ACSM offers specialty certifications for professionals seeking credentials to work with specific populations of individuals. For a list of all current ACSM certifications, visit www.acsm.org/certification.

Describe the Profile of an ACSM Certified Personal Trainer

An ACSM Certified Personal Trainer is a fitness professional who develops and implements an individualized approach to exercise leadership in healthy populations and/or those individuals who have medical clearance to exercise.

Using a variety of teaching techniques, the ACSM Certified Personal Trainer is proficient in

- Leading and demonstrating safe and effective methods of exercise by applying the fundamental principles of exercise science
- Writing appropriate exercise recommendations
- Motivating individuals to begin and continue with healthy behaviors

Eligibility

Candidates for ACSM certification must

- Have a high school diploma or equivalent
- Be 18 years of age or older
- Have a current adult CPR certification (with practical skills component)

Work Setting

ACSM Certified Personal Trainers work in health club, university, corporate, or community/public health settings.

Scope of Practice

The ACSM Certified Personal Trainer

- Works with healthy individuals or those who have medical clearance to exercise.
- Performs basic fitness assessments and field tests.
- Makes appropriate exercise recommendations.

Tell Me about the ACSM Exam

Here are some details:

Exam Specs

Duration: 2.5 hours
Number of Questions: 125–150

Exam Costs

One-day exam (for experienced professionals), $129
Three-day exam (for individuals who are new to the field), $375

Exam Languages

The exam is given in English, simplified Chinese, and Spanish.

Recommended Study Materials

- *ACSM's Resources for the Personal Trainer*
- *ACSM's Guidelines for Exercise Testing and Prescription*
- *ACSM's Certification Review*
- ACSM Learning Portal

Pass Rates

Seventy-one percent of 1,789 first-time candidates passed.

Any Tips for Exam Preparation?

There is a live tutorial on the ACSM Web site at www.acsm.org/certification that walks people through the testing experience. They can see how videos and photos are used on the exam as well as see practice questions.

Here are some other tips:

1. *Pick a date that allows you plenty of time to prepare.* The ACSM recommends that candidates choose a date three to six months in advance; however, candidates vary in their level of current education and study habits. Ultimately, what matters isn't how many months you spend, but rather the total number of hours you study.

2. *Purchase the recommended study materials.* Although this is not required, the ACSM strongly encourages all candidates to use its textbooks to prepare. Visit www.acsm.org/studymaterials to make sure you are studying the correct edition.

3. *Review the knowledge, skills, and abilities (KSAs).* These are found in any ACSM-recommended textbook. Each exam item is written about a KSA. Review the exam blueprint. Recognize the percentage of exam questions in each section. Compare the

KSAs for each section and determine which section(s) will need more review time. Find the chapters in the textbooks that correspond to the KSAs you need to study.

4. *Schedule or apply for your exam at www.pearsonvue.com/ ACSM.* By the time you schedule your exam, you should have a general idea of how much time you still need to spend studying. Don't worry if you need to reschedule; you can do so up to 24 hours in advance at no charge. If you are an RCEP candidate, you will need to apply (www.acsm.org/rcepapp) and be approved before you can schedule your exam.

5. *Participate in interactive study methods.* Sign up for an in-person workshop (www.acsm.org/register), participate in a live Webinar (www.acsm.org/certification), or take a course or practice test on the ACSM Learning Portal (www.acsm learning.org).

    As mentioned earlier, there is a live tutorial on the ACSM Web site that walks you through the testing experience.

6. *Attend ACSM Webinars.* You can learn from an ACSM expert from the convenience of your own home. As a Webinar participant, you will view a PowerPoint presentation live online and call in toll-free to join other professionals from all over the world in this learning experience.

    ACSM Webinars are interactive, and question-and-answer periods with the expert are provided. Audio recordings are provided to you following each Webinar. You may take one, two, or all of the Webinars available to help you prepare for the ACSM certification exam. To find course dates and times, visit www.acsm.org/register.

Exam Registration and Certification Information

To register for an ACSM exam, visit www.pearsonvue.com/acsm or call 1-888-883-2276. Exams are available on demand with immediate results. To receive more information about ACSM certification, visit www.acsm.org/certification.

What Are the Emphasis Areas for the ACSM Exam?

The ACSM recommends that all candidates review the free online candidate handbook available at www.acsm.org/candidatehandbook prior to taking an exam.

The emphasis areas (competency areas) for the Certified Personal Trainer exam and the approximate percentage of the exam that each represents are

Exercise physiology and related exercise science: 24%

Exercise prescription and programming: 28%

Human behavior: 4%

Health appraisal and fitness exercise testing: 13%

Safety, injury prevention, and emergency procedures: 8%

Nutrition and weight management: 9%

Patient management and medications: N/A

Program administration, quality assurance, and outcome assessment: 4%

Clinical and medical considerations (CPT only): 10%

Pathophysiology and risk factors: N/A

Electrocardiography and diagnostic techniques: N/A

Medical and surgical management: N/A

Physiology: diagnosis and treatment: N/A

Disability awareness: N/A

Americans with Disabilities Act (ADA) and facility design: N/A

Continuing Education

Continuing education is required by the ACSM to ensure ongoing competency and to maintain a high standard for ACSM-certified professionals. ACSM continuing education credit (CEC) requirements vary by certification.

Earning Continuing Education Credits

To ensure ongoing competency and to maintain a high standard for certified professionals, every ACSM credential is renewed on a three-year basis.

Certification/registration renewal is granted to candidates who successfully

Earn the required number of CECs *and*

Maintain a current CPR certification *and*

Pay the required three-year recertification/renewal fee.

Alternatively, the candidate has the option of repeating the certification examination for the particular level of certification for which he wishes to be recertified (if the exam is available and the candidate still meets the minimum requirements).

The total number of CECs and recertification/renewal fees required for each certification/registry level for a three-year period are 45 CECs and $30.

CECs can be earned in the following ways after you become certified:

1. Attending professional education meetings, or taking continuing education self-tests (such as those found in professional journals) that offer CECs, CMEs (continuing medical education), or continuing education units (CEUs) from the ACSM or other nationally recognized organizations

2. Taking and receiving a passing grade in a health/fitness or exercise science–related course from an accredited college or university that maintains or enhances professional development

3. Authoring or coauthoring published books or journal articles, or accepted abstracts

4. Teaching academic courses; conducting classroom instruction; or presenting health, fitness, or clinical lectures at an organized professional conference

5. Attending an ACSM certification workshop or an ACSM-endorsed meeting or program

6. Completing distance education or Internet continuing education programs on specific clinical or preventive topics

If you are attending a program that is not endorsed by the ACSM, please obtain CEC documentation. Examples of CEC documentation include an official continuing education certificate or a letter stating the number of CECs earned.

Audit Policies

At the time of recertification/renewal, you are required only to complete the online renewal form, but you must retain documented proof of all credits obtained for one year. ACSM will audit a percentage of randomly selected ACSM renewals. If you are audited, you will be required to provide documented proof of all credits to the ACSM National Office within 30 days.

Certification and Registry Status

You are considered ACSM certified or registered during the three years for which your credential is current. If you do not recertify, you are no longer considered ACSM certified or registered. If you are no longer ACSM certified or registered, you may not claim to be ACSM certified or registered.

ACSM Sample Test Questions

Clinical Comprehensive Examination

(Answers can be found at the end of the clinical comprehensive section.)

DIRECTIONS: Each of the numbered items or incomplete statements in this section is followed by answers or by completions of the statement. Select the ONE lettered answer or completion that is BEST in each case.

1. If a healthy young man who weighs 80 kg exercises at an intensity of 45 mL $\cdot$ kg–1 $\cdot$ min–1 for 30 minutes, five times per week, how long would it take him to lose 10 pounds of fat?

   A. 9 weeks
   B. 11 weeks
   C. 13 weeks
   D. 15 weeks

2. For previously sedentary individuals, a 20% to 30% reduction in all-cause mortality can be obtained from physical activity with a daily energy expenditure of

   A. 50 to 80 kcal/day.
   B. 80 to 100 kcal/day.
   C. 150 to 200 kcal/day.
   D. >400 kcal/day.

3. Which of the following is an example of physical activity requiring anaerobic glycolysis to produce energy in the form of adenosine triphosphate (ATP)?

   A. 400-m sprint
   B. 2-mi run

C. 100-m sprint

D. All of the above

4. Healthy, untrained individuals have an anaerobic threshold at approximately what percentage of their maximal oxygen consumption (VO_2 max)?

A. 25%

B. 55%

C. 75%

D. 95%

5. A 35-year-old female client asks the Exercise Specialist to estimate her energy expenditure. She weighs 110 lb and pedals the cycle ergometer at 50 rpm with a resistance of 2.5 kp for 60 minutes. The Specialist should report which of the following caloric values?

A. 250 calories

B. 510 calories

C. 770 calories

D. 1,700 calories

6. What is the total caloric equivalent of 3.0 lb (1.36 kg) of fat?

A. 1,000 kcal

B. 5,500 kcal

C. 10,500 kcal

D. 15,000 kcal

7. The breakdown of _____ would be described as the energy used to perform physical work in a short time interval (5 to 10 seconds).

A. testosterone

B. oxygen

C. ATP

D. phosphocreatine

8. An aerobic exercise prescription of 5 days per week at 50% to 85% of maximal oxygen consumption (VO_2 max) for 45 minutes will most favorably affect which of the following blood lipid profiles?

A. Lipoprotein (a)

B. Triglycerides

C. Total cholesterol

D. Low-density lipoprotein cholesterol

9. A _____ period redistributes blood flow from the trunk to peripheral areas, decreases resistance in the tissues, and increases tissue temperature and energy production.

A. training

B. cool-down

C. warm-up

D. detraining

10. A balance between the energy required by the working muscles and the rate of ATP production during exercise is referred to as

A. anaerobic cellular respiration.

B. oxygen debt.

C. oxygen deficit.

D. steady state.

11. What is the relative oxygen consumption rate for walking on a treadmill at 3.5 mph with a 10% grade?

A. 18.17 mL · kg–1 · min–1

B. 27.96 mL · kg–1 · min–1

C. 29.76 mL · kg–1 · min–1

D. 31.28 mL · kg–1 · min–1

12. Advanced aging causes a progressive decline in which of the following?

A. Bone density

B. Bone distensibility

C. Bone fractures

D. None of the above

13. At exercise intensities up to 50% of maximal oxygen consumption, what facilitates an increase in cardiac output?

A. Heart rate and stroke volume

B. Heart rate only

C. Stroke volume only

D. Neither heart rate nor stroke volume

14. Which of the following refers to a muscular contraction sustained against a fixed load or resistance with no change in the joint angle?

A. Eccentric load

B. Isokinetic contraction

C. Isometric contraction

D. Isotonic contraction

15. What is the total energy expenditure for a 70-kg man doing an exercise session composed of 5 minutes of warm-up at 2.0 METs, 20 minutes of treadmill running at 9 METs, 20 minutes of leg cycling at 8 METs, and 5 minutes of cool down at 2.5 METs?

A. 162 kcal

B. 868 kcal

C. 444 kcal

D. 1,256 kcal

16. What is the cardiac output at maximal exercise with a heart rate of 200 beats/min and stroke volume of 100 mL/beat?

A. 5 L/min

B. 10 L/min

C. 20 L/min

D. 20 mL/min

17. How should the exercise prescription be initially altered for a patient exercising in the heat or in a humid environment?

    A. Increasing the intensity and increasing the duration
    B. Decreasing the intensity and increasing the duration
    C. Decreasing the intensity and decreasing the duration
    D. Increasing the intensity and decreasing the duration

18. Which of the following methods CANNOT measure oxygen consumption?

    A. Direct calorimetry
    B. Indirect calorimetry
    C. Estimation from workload
    D. Pulmonary function testing

19. What is the sum of the oxygen cost of physical activity and the resting energy expenditure called?

    A. Relative oxygen consumption
    B. Absolute oxygen consumption
    C. Net oxygen consumption
    D. Gross oxygen consumption

20. Which exercise intensity is used for training muscular endurance?

A. 10% to 40% of one repetition maximum

B. 20% to 40% of one repetition maximum

C. 40% to 60% of one repetition maximum

D. 60% to 80% of one repetition maximum

21. A regular exercise program will have what effect?

A. Increase myocardial oxygen cost for a given submaximal exercise intensity

B. Increase serum high-density lipoprotein cholesterol; decrease serum triglycerides

C. Reduce exercise threshold for the accumulation of lactate in the blood

D. Increase total cholesterol–low-density cholesterol ratio

22. Cardiorespiratory endurance, resistance, and flexibility programming are indicative of which phase of an exercise prescription?

A. Stimulus phase

B. Warm-up

C. Cool-down

D. Resistance training

23. Which of the following is the best example of physical activity requiring aerobic metabolism to produce ATP?

A. 40-yard dash

B. 400-m sprint

C. 5,000-m run

D. Marathon run

Clinical Comprehensive Examination Answers and Explanations

1. C. The steps are as follows:

   A. Convert relative VO_2 to absolute VO_2 by multiplying relative VO_2 ($mL \cdot kg-1 \cdot min-1$) by his body weight.

   B. The young man weighs 80 kg. Therefore, absolute VO_2 = relative VO_2 × body weight = 45 $mL \cdot kg-1 \cdot min-1$ × 80 kg = 3,600 $mL \cdot min-1$.

   C. To get $L \cdot min-1$, divide $mL \cdot min-1$ by 1,000:
      3,600 $mL \cdot min-1$ ÷ 1,000 = 3.60 $L \cdot min-1$

   D. Multiply 3.60 $L \cdot min-1$ by the constant 5.0 to get $kcal \cdot min-1$:
      3.60 $L \cdot min-1$ × 5.0 = 18.0 $kcal \cdot min-1$

   E. Multiply 18.0 $kcal \cdot min-1$ by the total number of minutes that he exercises (30 minutes × 5 times per week = 150 total minutes) to get the total caloric expenditure:
      18.0 $kcal \cdot min-1$ × 150 minutes = 2,700 kcal per week

   F. Divide by 3,500 to get pounds of fat:
      2,700 kcal/week ÷ 3,500 kcal/lb of fat
      = 0.7714 lb of fat/week

   G. Divide 10 lb by 0.7714 to get how many weeks it will take him to lose 10 lb of fat: 10 lb of fat ÷ 0.7714 = 12.96 weeks or approximately 13.0 weeks.

2. C. A minimal caloric threshold of 150 to 200 kcal of physical activity per day is associated with a significant 20% to 30% reduction in risk of all-cause mortality, and this should be the initial goal for previously sedentary individuals.

3. A. A 400-meter sprint is an example of physical activity requiring anaerobic glycolysis to produce energy in the form of ATP. A 100-meter sprint requires rapid energy by transferring high-energy phosphate from creatine phosphate to rephosphorylate ATP. The 2-mile run will utilize oxidative phosphorylation for ATP production.

4. B. A healthy, unconditioned person has an anaerobic threshold of approximately 55% of maximal oxygen consumption. A conditioned person can have an anaerobic threshold as high as 70% to 90% of maximal oxygen consumption. The onset of metabolic acidosis or anaerobic metabolism can be measured through serial measurements of blood lactate level or assessment of expired gases, specifically pulmonary ventilation and carbon dioxide production.

5. B. The steps are as follows:

    A. Choose the ACSM leg cycling formula.
    B. Write down your knowns, and convert the values to the appropriate units:
        110 lb ÷ 2.2 = 50 kg; 50 rpm × 6 m = 300 m · min–1; 2.5 kp = 2.5kg; 60 minutes of cycling

C. Write down the ACSM leg cycling formula:

Leg cycling $(mL \cdot kg{-}1 \cdot min{-}1)$

$= (1.8 \times \text{work rate} \div \text{body weight}) + 3.5 + 3.5$ $(mL \cdot kg{-}1 \cdot min{-}1)$

D. Calculate the work rate:

Work rate $= kg \cdot m \cdot min{-}1 = 2.5\ kg \cdot 300\ m \cdot min{-}1$

$= 750\ kg \cdot m \cdot min{-}1$

E. Substitute the known values for the variable name:

$mL \cdot kg{-}1 \cdot min{-}1 = (1.8 \times 750 \div 50) + 3.5 + 3.5$

F. Solve for the unknown:

$mL \cdot kg{-}1 \cdot min{-}1 = 27 + 3.5 + 3.5$

Gross leg cycling $VO_2 = 34\ mL \cdot kg{-}1 \cdot min{-}1$

G. To find out how many calories she expends, we must first convert her oxygen consumption to absolute terms:

Absolute VO_2 = relative VO_2 × body weight

$= 34\ mL \cdot kg{-}1 \cdot min{-}1 \times 50\ kg = 1,700\ mL \cdot min{-}1$

H. Convert $mL \cdot min{-}1$ to $L \cdot min{-}1$ by dividing by 1,000:

$1,700\ mL \cdot min{-}1 \div 1,000 = 1.7\ L \cdot min{-}1$

I. Next, we must see how many calories she expends in 1 minute by multiplying her absolute VO_2 (in $L \cdot min{-}1$) by the constant 5.0:

$1.7\ L \cdot min{-}1 \times 5.0 = 8.5\ kcal \cdot min{-}1$

J. Finally, multiply the number of calories she expends in 1 minute by the number of minutes that she cycles:

$8.5\ kcal \cdot min{-}1 \times 60\ \text{minutes} = 510$ total calories.

6. C. To convert from pounds of fat to total kilocalories, multiply the fat weight (in pounds) by 3,500. The correct answer is 3 × 3,500 = 10,500 kcal.

7. C. The energy to perform physical work comes from the breakdown of ATP. The amount of directly available ATP is small, with action lasting only 5 to 10 seconds; thus, ATP must be resynthesized constantly.

8. B. Triglycerides are the only substance listed that has been proved to be directly affected by exercise. Lipoprotein (a) has not been shown to change favorably with exercise. Low-density lipoprotein cholesterol and total cholesterol are affected by diet and may be lowered indirectly by weight loss associated with exercise.

9. C. Warm-up exercises tend to redistribute blood flow from the trunk to peripheral areas, decrease resistance in the tissues for movement, and increase tissue temperature and energy production. Cool-down exercises have the opposite effect.

10. D. At exercise, a steady-state condition occurs when a balance exists between the energy required by the working muscles and the rate of ATP production through aerobic cellular respiration or aerobic metabolism. Anaerobic cellular respiration is a series of ATP-producing reactions that do not require oxygen. Oxygen debt is the oxygen consumption in excess of the resting oxygen consumption at the end of an exercise session. Oxygen deficit is the difference between total oxygen actually consumed and the amount that would have been consumed in a steady state.

11. C. The steps are as follows:

A. Choose the ACSM walking formula.

B. Write down your knowns, and convert the values to the appropriate units:

3.5mph × 26.8 = 93.8 m · min−1; 10% grade = 0.10

C. Write down the ACSM walking formula:

Walking (kg−1 · min−1) = (0.1 × speed) + (1.8 × speed × fractional grade) + 3.5 (mL · kg−1 · min−1)

D. Substitute the known values for the variable name:

mL · kg−1 · min−1 = (0.1 × 93.8) + (1.8 × 93.8 × 0.1) + 3.5
mL · kg−1 · min−1 = 9.38 + 16.884 + 3.5

E. Solve for the unknown:

mL · kg−1 · min−1 = 9.38 + 16.884 + 3.5
Gross walking VO_2 = 29.76 mL · kg−1 · min−1

12. A. Advanced aging brings about a progressive decline in bone mineral density and calcium homeostasis. This loss accelerates in women immediately after menopause. As a result, older people, especially women, are at increased risk for bone fractures, which are a significant cause of morbidity and mortality. Hip fractures are the most common type and account for a large share of the disabilities, death, and high medical costs associated with accidents and falls.

13. A. At exercise intensities up to 50% of maximal oxygen consumption, the increase in cardiac output is facilitated by increases in heart rate and stroke volume. Thereafter, the increase results almost solely from the continued rise in heart rate.

14. C. An isometric contraction occurs when a muscle group contracts against a fixed load with no apparent movement or no change in joint angle. An isotonic contraction makes a joint angle decrease or increase according to the movements and production of muscle forces. Isokinetic contractions refer to either concentric or eccentric contractions. An isokinetic contraction occurs at a fixed speed of movement and usually involves use of an isokinetic device that controls the speed of rotation along a joint's entire range of motion. An eccentric load is an amount of resistance applied directly to a muscle or muscle group during an eccentric contraction.

15. C. First determine the MET level for each activity:

Warm-up is 2.0 METs × 5 minutes = 10 METs

Treadmill is 9.0 METs × 20 minutes = 180 METs
   Cycle is 8.0

METs × 20 minutes = 160 METs

Cool-down is 2.5 METs × 5 minutes = 12.5 METs

Then determine the total number of METs for all activities: 10 + 180 + 160 + 12.5 = 362.5 METs.

Multiply 362.5 METs by 3.5 (because 1 MET = 3.5 mL · kg–1 · min–1), which equals 1,268.75 mL · kg–1.

Multiply 1,268.75 mL · kg–1 by body weight (70 kg), which equals 88,812.5 mL. Divide that number by 1,000 (because 1,000 mL = 1 L), which equals 88.81 L. Multiply 88.81 L by 5 (because 5 kcal equals 1 L of oxygen consumed), which equals 444 kcal.

16. C. Cardiac output (CO) is the product of stroke volume times heart rate.

$$CO = (100 \text{ mL} \cdot \text{beat–1}) \cdot (200 \text{ beats} \cdot \text{min–1})$$

Convert mL to L by dividing by 1,000, which gives 20 L · min–1.

17. C. High ambient temperature or relative humidity increases the risk of heat-related disorders, including heat cramps, heat syncope, dehydration, heat exhaustion, and heat stroke. In this type of environment, the exercise prescription should be altered by initially lowering both the intensity and the duration of exercise to allow for acclimation.

18. D. Oxygen consumption can be measured in the laboratory using techniques of direct and indirect calorimetry, or it can be estimated from the workload. Pulmonary function testing is used to identify pulmonary disorders, such as restrictive and obstructive pulmonary disease.

19. D. Individuals require approximately 3.5 mL · kg–1· min–1 (1 MET) of oxygen at rest. Physical activity elevates oxygen consumption above resting levels. Net oxygen consumption is the

difference between the oxygen consumption value for exercise and the resting value. Net oxygen consumption is used to assess the caloric cost of exercise. Gross oxygen consumption is the sum of the oxygen cost of the physical activity and the resting component. Net and gross oxygen consumption can be expressed in relative or absolute terms.

20. C. Rapid strength gains will be achieved at higher resistance or weight (80% to 100% of one repetition maximum) and a lower number of repetitions (six to eight). For muscular endurance, a lower weight is used (40% to 60% of one repetition maximum) with a higher number of repetitions—usually 8 to 15.

21. B. Regular physical activity and/or exercise reduces coronary artery disease risk by increasing serum high-density lipoprotein cholesterol and decreasing serum triglycerides.

22. A. The stimulus (conditioning) phase includes cardiorespiratory endurance, resistance, and flexibility programming.

23. D. The 400-m sprint is an example of physical activity requiring anaerobic glycolysis to produce energy in the form of ATP. Shorter sprints rely on ready stores of ATP and phosphocreatine. Longer runs require aerobic metabolism to produce ATP.

Health and Fitness Comprehensive Examination

(Answers can be found at the end of the health and fitness section.)

Each of the numbered items or incomplete statements in this section is followed by answers or by completions of the statement. Select the ONE lettered answer or completion that is BEST in each case.

24. Which of the following represents more than 90% of the fat stored in the body and is composed of a glycerol molecule connected to three fatty acids?
    A. Phospholipids
    B. Cholesterol
    C. Triglycerides
    D. Free fatty acids

25. Calcium, phosphorus, magnesium, potassium, sulfur, sodium, and chloride are examples of
    A. macrominerals.
    B. microminerals.
    C. proteins.
    D. vitamins.

26. Which of the following terms represents an imaginary horizontal plane passing through the midsection of the body and dividing it into upper and lower portions?

    A. Sagittal
    B. Frontal
    C. Transverse
    D. Superior

27. Moving the hand from palm up to palm down with the elbow flexed at 90 degrees

   A. adducts the ulna.
   B. internally rotates the radius.
   C. internally rotates the humerus.
   D. flexes the ulna.

28. Which of the following energy systems is capable of using all three fuels (carbohydrates, fats, and proteins)?

   A. Anaerobic glycolysis
   B. Lactic acid system
   C. Phosphagen system
   D. Aerobic system

29. Anaerobic glycolysis is also known as the

   A. phosphagen system.
   B. aerobic metabolism.
   C. lactic acid system.
   D. none of the above.

30. Muscle fibers that can produce a large amount of tension in a very short period of time but fatigue quickly are referred to as:

   A. slow-twitch glycolytic.
   B. fast-twitch glycolytic.

C. fast-twitch oxidative.

D. slow-twitch oxidative.

31. Rotation of the anterior surface of a bone toward the midline of the body is called

A. medial rotation.

B. lateral rotation.

C. supination.

D. pronation.

32. Which of the following water-soluble vitamins must be consumed on a daily basis?

A. Vitamins A and C

B. Vitamins A, D, E, and K

C. Vitamin B complex and C

D. Vitamins A, B complex, D, and K

33. An individual's maximal oxygen consumption (VO_2 max) is a measure of the power of the aerobic energy system. This value is generally regarded as the best indicator of aerobic fitness. At what percentage of one's VO_2 max does the anaerobic threshold occur in untrained individuals?

A. 55%

B. 65%

C. 75%

D. 85%

34. What type of muscle tissue is the most abundant in the body?

    A. Arteries
    B. Cardiac
    C. Skeletal
    D. Smooth

35. Which of the following is NOT true regarding the psychological benefits of regular exercise in the elderly?

    A. Self-concept
    B. Life satisfaction
    C. Stimulate appetite
    D. Self-efficacy

36. When exercise training children,

    A. exercise programs should increase physical fitness in the short term and strength and stamina in the long term.
    B. strength training should be avoided for safety reasons.
    C. increasing the rate of training intensity more than approximately 10% per week increases the likelihood of overuse injuries of bone.
    D. children with exercise-induced asthma are often unable to lead active lives.

37. Which of the following types of muscle stretching can cause residual muscle soreness, is time consuming, and typically requires a partner?

A. Static

B. Ballistic

C. Proprioceptive neuromuscular facilitation

D. All of the above

38. Glucose, fructose, and sucrose are commonly referred to as

A. proteins.

B. complex carbohydrates.

C. simple carbohydrates.

D. fats.

39. All energy for muscular contraction must come from the breakdown of a chemical compound called

A. adenosine triphosphate (ATP).

B. guanosine triphosphate (GTP).

C. nicotinamide adenine dinucleotide (NAD).

D. flavin adenine dinucleotide (FADH2).

40. What two regulatory proteins are found within the actin complex of skeletal muscle?

A. Epimysium and perimysium

B. Perimysium and endomysium

C. Troponin and tropomyosin

D. Myosin and troponin

41. A body weight of 15% less than expected, a morbid fear of fat-ness, a preoccupation with food, and an abnormal body image are symptoms of

    A. Bulimia nervosa.
    B. Dieting.
    C. Anorexia nervosa.
    D. Obesity.

42. The process of adding a second stimulus to a muscle fiber that has already been excited is known as

    A. twitch.
    B. tetanus.
    C. summation.
    D. motor unit.

43. The ACSM recommendation for intensity, duration, and fre-quency of cardiorespiratory exercise for apparently healthy individuals includes

    A. intensity of 60% to 90% maximal heart rate, duration of 20 to 60 minutes, and frequency of 3 to 5 days a week.
    B. intensity of 85% to 90% maximal heart rate, duration of 30 minutes, and frequency of 3 days a week.
    C. intensity of 50% to 70% maximal heart rate, duration of 15 to 45 minutes, and frequency of 5 days a week.

D. intensity of 60% to 90% maximal heart rate reserve, duration of 20 to 60 minutes, and frequency of 7 days a week.

44. A method of strength and power training that involves an
eccentric loading of muscles and tendons followed immediately
by an explosive concentric contraction is called

A. plyometrics.
B. periodization.
C. super-sets.
D. isotonic reversals.

45. Sufficient ATP is stored in a given skeletal muscle to fuel how
many seconds of activity?

A. 2 to 3
B. 5 to 10
C. 10 to 20
D. 45 to 60

46. The sliding filament theory of muscle contraction depends on
the interaction of the contractile proteins actin and myosin.
At rest, no interaction occurs. When the muscle is called on
to contract, these two proteins create an interdigitation, and
the muscle then contracts. This process is dependent on the
presence of

A. magnesium.
B. manganese.

C. creatine.

D. calcium.

47. A measure of muscular endurance is

   A. one-repetition maximum.

   B. three-repetition maximum.

   C. number of curl-ups in 1 minute.

   D. number of curl-ups in 3 minutes.

48. The ACSM recommends that exercise intensity be prescribed within what percentage of maximal heart rate range?

   A. 40% and 60%

   B. 50% and 80%

   C. 60% and 90%

   D. 70% and 100%

49. The ACSM recommends how many repetitions of each exercise for muscular strength and endurance?

   A. 5 to 6

   B. 8 to 12

   C. 12 to 20

   D. More than 20

50. Which of the following are changes seen as a result of regular, chronic exercise?

A. Decreased heart rate at rest

B. Increased stroke volume at rest

C. No change in cardiac output at rest

D. All of the above

51. Fitness assessment is an important aspect of the training program because it provides information for which of the following?

A. Developing the exercise prescription

B. Evaluating proper nutritional choices

C. Diagnosing musculoskeletal injury

D. Developing appropriate billing categories

52. Following an acute musculoskeletal injury, the appropriate action calls for stabilization of the area and incorporating the RICE treatment method. RICE is the acronym for which of the following?

A. Recovery, Ibuprofen, Compression, Education

B. Rest and Ice for injury Care

C. Rest, Ice, Compression, Elevation

D. Rotate, Ice, Care, Evaluate

53. A resistance training program that starts with light weights and high repetitions for the first set and then gradually moves to heavier weights and fewer repetitions for each

successive set would be an example of which of the following training styles?

A. Circuits
B. Super-sets
C. Split routines
D. Pyramids

54. Which of the following activities provides the greatest improvement in aerobic fitness for someone who is beginning an exercise program?

A. Weight training
B. Downhill snow skiing
C. Stretching
D. Walking

55. Generally, low-fit or sedentary persons may benefit from

A. shorter duration, higher intensity, and higher frequency of exercise.
B. longer duration, higher intensity, and higher frequency of exercise.
C. shorter duration, lower intensity, and higher frequency of exercise.
D. shorter duration, higher intensity, and lower frequency of exercise.

24. C. Dietary fats include triglycerides, sterols (e.g., cholesterol), and phospholipids. Triglycerides represent more than 90% of the fat stored in the body. A triglyceride is a glycerol molecule connected to three fatty acid molecules. The fatty acids are identified by the amount of "saturation," or the number of single or double bonds that link the carbon atoms. Saturated fatty acids have only single bonds. Monounsaturated fatty acids have one double bond, and polyunsaturated fatty acids have two or more double bonds.

25. A. Minerals are inorganic substances that perform a variety of functions in the body. Many play an important role in assisting enzymes (or coenzymes) that are necessary for the proper functioning of body systems. They also are found in cell membranes, hormones, muscles, and connective tissues as well as electrolytes in body fluids. Minerals are considered to be either macrominerals (needed in relatively large doses), such as calcium, phosphorus, magnesium, potassium, sulfur, sodium, and chloride, or microminerals (needed in very small amounts), such as iron, zinc, selenium, manganese, molybdenum, iodine, copper, chromium, and fluoride.

26. C. The body has three cardinal planes, and each individual plane is perpendicular to the other two. Movement occurs along these planes. The sagittal plane divides the body into

right and left parts, and the midsagittal plane is represented by an imaginary vertical plane passing through the midline of the body, dividing it into right and left halves. The frontal plane is represented by an imaginary vertical plane passing through the body, dividing it into front and back halves. The transverse plane represents an imaginary horizontal plane passing through the midsection of the body and dividing it into upper and lower portions.

27. B. Rotation is a movement of long bones about their long axis. Angular movements decrease or increase the joint angle produced by the articulating bones. The four types of angular movements are flexion (a movement that decreases the joint angle, bringing the bones closer together), extension (the movement opposite to flexion that decreases the joint angle between two bones), abduction (the movement of a body part away from the midline in a lateral direction), and adduction (the opposite of abduction, the movement toward the midline of the body).

28. D. The oxygen system is capable of using all three fuels (carbohydrate, fat, and protein). However, significant amounts of protein are not used as a source of ATP energy during most types of exercise. Although all three fuels can be used, the two most important are carbohydrate and fat. When fat is used as a fuel, significantly more energy is released; however, this requires that more oxygen be supplied to produce this energy. If proteins are used, the amount of energy is comparable to that of carbohydrate. The carbohydrate, fat, and small amount of protein used

by this energy system during exercise are metabolized completely, leaving only carbon dioxide (which is exhaled) and water. The nitrogen found in the protein is excreted as urea.

29. C. Anaerobic glycolysis is also known as the lactic acid system. A human stores carbohydrate in the body as muscle (or liver) glycogen. Glycogen is simply a long string of glucose molecules hooked end to end. Anaerobic glycolysis can use only carbohydrate, not fat or protein, as fuel. This system will use muscle glycogen, which is broken down to glucose and then enters anaerobic glycolysis.

    Only a small amount of ATP is produced, and the end product is lactic acid (or lactate). If lactate is allowed to accumulate significantly in the muscle, it eventually will cause fatigue. Because no oxygen is required, this system is anaerobic.

30. B. Fast-twitch (type II) muscle fibers can be subdivided into fast-twitch aerobic (type IIa) and fast-twitch glycolytic (type IIb). Although it is classified as a fast-twitch fiber, the type IIa fiber has the capability to perform some amounts of aerobic work. The motor nerve supplying fast-twitch fibers is larger than the supplying slow-twitch muscle fibers. Fast-twitch fibers are recruited when performing high-intensity, short-duration activities. Examples include weightlifting, sprints, jumping, and other similar activities. These fibers can produce large amounts of tension in a very short period; however, they fatigue quickly.

31. A. Rotation is the turning of a bone around its own longitudinal axis or around another bone. Rotation of the anterior sur-

face of the bone toward the midline of the body is medial rotation, whereas rotation of the same bone away from the midline is lateral rotation. Supination is a specialized rotation of the forearm that results in the palm of the hand being turned forward (anteriorly).

Pronation (the opposite of supination) is the rotation of the forearm that results in the palm of the hand being directed backward (posteriorly).

32. C. The fat-soluble vitamins are vitamins A, D, E, and K; they are stored in body fat after consumption. Vitamins C and B complex are water-soluble vitamins and must be consumed on a regular basis; excess amounts are excreted. Water-soluble vitamins are found in citrus fruits, broccoli, cauliflower, brussels sprouts, whole-grain breads and cereals, and organ meats. They serve as antioxidants as well as coenzymes in carbohydrate metabolism, metabolic pathways, amino acid metabolism, and nucleic acid metabolism.

33. A. The oxygen system is complicated and involves many reactions. The oxygen system takes 2 to 3 minutes to adjust to a new exercise intensity. This system is ranked third in power. An individual's VO_2 max is a measure of the power of the aerobic energy system. This value generally is regarded as the best indicator of aerobic fitness. Training adaptations are evident in the exercise intensity at which the anaerobic threshold occurs. In untrained individuals, the anaerobic threshold occurs at 55% of a person's VO_2 max. In well-trained endurance athletes, the anaerobic threshold occurs at 80% to 85% of their VO_2 max.

34. C. Skeletal muscle tissue enables movement of the body and is composed of individual cells known as myocytes or myofibers. Skeletal muscle tissue accounts for nearly 50% of the body's muscle mass and is the most abundant muscle tissue in the body. Cardiac muscle tissue, also known as heart muscle, pumps blood through the circulatory system. Smooth muscle tissue assists in the regulation of blood flow to various parts of the body.

35. C. Older people who exercise regularly report greater life satisfaction (older people who exercise regularly have a more positive attitude toward their work and generally are in better health than sedentary persons), greater happiness (strong correlations have been reported between the activity level of older adults and self-reported happiness), higher self-efficacy (older persons taking part in exercise programs commonly report that they can do everyday tasks more easily than before they began exercising), improved self-concept and self-esteem (older adults improve their score on self-concept questionnaires following participation in an exercise program), and reduced psychological stress (exercise is effective in reducing psychological stress without unwanted side effects).

36. C. Increasing the rate of progression of training more than approximately 10% per week is a risk factor for overuse injuries of bone. Exercise programs for children and adolescents should increase physical fitness in the short term and lead to adoption of a physically active lifestyle in the long term.

Strength training in youth carries no greater risk of injury than comparable strength training programs in adults if proper instruction, exercise prescription, and supervision are provided. Children who have exercise-induced asthma often are physically unfit because of restriction of activity imposed by the child, parents, or physicians.

37. C. Three different stretching techniques typically are practiced and have associated risks and benefits. Static stretching is the most commonly recommended approach to stretching. It involves slowly stretching a muscle to the point of individual discomfort and holding that position for a period of 10 to 30 seconds. Minimal risk of injury exists, and it has been shown to be effective.

Ballistic stretching uses repetitive bouncing-type movements to produce muscle stretch. These movements can produce residual muscle soreness or acute injury. Proprioceptive neuromuscular facilitation stretching alternates contraction and relaxation of both agonist and antagonist muscle groups. This technique is effective, but it can cause residual muscle soreness and is time consuming.

Additionally, a partner typically is required, and the potential for injury exists when the partner-assisted stretching is applied too vigorously.

38. C. Carbohydrates are compounds made of carbon, hydrogen, and oxygen. They are commonly known as simple carbohydrates (sugars) or complex carbohydrates (starch). Glucose, fructose, and sucrose are examples of sugars or simple carbohy-

drates. Some sources are refined sugar (white or brown) and fruits. Food sources for complex carbohydrates are grains, breads, cereals, pastas, potatoes, beans, and legumes. Proteins have nitrogen in them as well as carbon, hydrogen, and oxygen and may be found in such food sources as meats and nuts. Fats are found in foods such as butter and oils.

39. A. All energy for muscular contraction must come from the breakdown of ATP. The energy is stored in the bonds between the last two phosphates. When work is performed (e.g., a biceps curl), the last phosphate is split (forming ADP), releasing heat energy. Some (but not all) of this heat energy is converted to mechanical energy to perform the curl. Because humans are not 100% efficient at converting this heat energy to mechanical energy, the rest of the heat is released to the environment.

40. C. A muscle is composed of muscle fibers (or cells). Each muscle fiber is composed of many myofibrils. Each myofibril is composed of sarcomeres.

The sarcomere is the smallest part of muscle that can contract. The contractile (or muscle) proteins are contained in the sarcomere. Actin is a muscle protein (sometimes called the thin filament) that can be visualized as a twisted strand of beads. Actin also contains two other proteins, troponin and tropomyosin. Tropomyosin is a long, stringlike molecule that wraps around the actin filament. Troponin is a specialized protein found at the ends of the tropomyosin filament.

41. C. Disordered eating covers a continuum from preoccupation with food and body image to the syndromes of anorexia nervosa and bulimia. Anorexia nervosa is defined by symptoms that include a body weight that is 15% less than expected, a morbid fear of being or becoming fat, a preoccupation with food, and an abnormal body image (the thin person feels "fat"). Bulimia nervosa is defined by symptoms that include binge eating twice a week for at least 3 months, loss of control over eating, purging behavior, and being overly concerned with body weight. Although specific psychiatric criteria must be met for a diagnosis to be made by a specialist, any degree of disordered eating can affect the eating pattern of the exerciser and place her or him at risk for nutritional deficiencies.

42. C. A motor unit consists of the efferent (motor) nerve and all muscle fibers supplied (or innervated) by that nerve. The total number of motor units varies among different muscles. In addition, the total number of fibers in each motor unit varies between and within muscles. Different degrees of contraction can be achieved by varying the total number of motor units stimulated (or recruited) in a particular muscle. The major determinants of how much force is produced when a muscle contracts are the number of motor units that are recruited and the number of muscle fibers in each motor unit. When a motor unit is stimulated by a single nerve impulse, it responds by contracting one time and then relaxing. This is called a twitch. If a motor unit is continuously stimulated without adequate time for relaxation to occur, tetanus occurs. If a motor unit receives a second stimula-

tion before it is allowed to relax, the two impulses are added (or summated), and the tension developed is greater.

43. A. The ability to take in and utilize oxygen is dependent on the health and integrity of the heart, lungs, and circulatory system. Efficiency of the aerobic metabolic pathways also is necessary to optimize cardiorespiratory fitness. The degree of improvement that may be expected in cardiorespiratory fitness is related directly to the frequency, intensity, duration, and mode or type of exercise. Maximal oxygen uptake may improve between 5% and 30% with training. The exercise prescription can be altered for different populations to achieve the same results. However, for an apparently healthy person, the ACSM recommends an intensity of 60% to 90% maximal heart rate, duration of 20 to 60 minutes, and frequency of 3 to 5 days a week.

44. A. Plyometrics is a method of strength and power training that involves an eccentric loading of muscles and tendons, followed immediately by an explosive concentric contraction. This stretch–shortening cycle may allow an enhanced generation of force during the concentric (shortening) phase. Most well-controlled studies have shown no significant difference in power improvement when comparing plyometrics with high-intensity strength training. The explosive nature of this type of activity may increase the risk for musculoskeletal injury. Plyometrics should not be considered a practical resistance exercise alternative for health/fitness applications, but it may be appropriate for select athletic or performance needs.

45. B. The stores of ATP energy in skeletal muscle are very limited (5 to 10 seconds of high-intensity work). After this time, another high-energy source, PC, which has only one high-energy phosphate band, begins to break down. The energy from the breakdown of PC is used to re-form ATP, which then breaks down to provide energy for exercise. Only energy released from the breakdown of ATP, however, can provide energy for biologic work such as exercise.

46. D. The sliding filament theory defines how skeletal muscles are believed to contract. These steps can best be described as what occurs during rest, stimulation, contraction, and then relaxation of the muscle. At rest, no nerve activity (except normal resting tone) occurs. Calcium is stored in a network of tubes in the muscle called the sarcoplasmic reticulum. If no calcium is present, the active sites (where the myosin cross-bridges can attach) are kept covered. If the active sites are uncovered, the enzyme that causes ATP to break down and release energy is kept inactive. During conditions when a nerve impulse is present, this impulse causes calcium to be released. The calcium binds to the troponin on the actin filament. When this occurs, the active sites are uncovered. Now, the myosin cross-bridges bind the active sites and form actomyosin (a connection between the actin and myosin proteins), and contraction occurs.

47. C. Three common assessments for muscular endurance include the bench press, for upper body endurance (a weight is lifted in cadence with a metronome or other timing device; the total

number of lifts performed correctly and in time with the cadence is measured); the push-up, for upper body endurance (the client assumes a standardized beginning position with the body held rigid and supported by the hands and toes for men and the hands and knees for women; the body is lowered to the floor, then pushed back up to the starting position; the score is the total number of properly performed push-ups completed without a pause by the client, with no time limit); and the curl-up (crunch), for abdominal muscular endurance (the client begins in the bent knee sit-up with knees at 90 degrees, the arms at the side, palms facing down with middle fingers touching masking tape. A second piece of tape is placed 10 cm apart; *or* set a metronome to 50 bpm and the client performs slow, controlled curl-ups to lift the shoulder blades off the mat with the trunk making a 30-degree angle, in time with the metronome at a rate of 25 per minute done for 1 minute; *or* the client performs as many curl-ups as possible in 1 minute.

48. C. Several methods for defining exercise intensity objectively are available. The ACSM recommends that exercise intensity be prescribed within a range of 64% to 70% and 94% of maximal heart rate or between 40% to 50% and 85% of oxygen uptake reserve (VO_2 maxr). Lower intensities will elicit a favorable response in individuals with very low fitness levels. Because of the variability in estimating maximal heart rate from age, it is recommended that, whenever possible, an actual maximal heart rate from a graded exercise test be used. Factors to consider when determining appropriate exercise intensity include age, fitness level, medications, overall health status, and individual goals.

49. B. The ACSM recommends that one set of 8 to 12 repetitions of each exercise should be performed to volitional fatigue for healthy individuals. Choose a range of repetitions between 3 and 20 (i.e., 3 to 5, 8 to 10, 10 to 15) that can be performed at a moderate repetition duration (3 seconds concentric, 3 seconds eccentric) based on age, fitness level, assessment, and ability. The ACSM recommends exercising each muscle group 2 to 3 nonconsecutive days per week.

50. D. The effects of regular (chronic) exercise can be classified or grouped into those that occur at rest, during moderate (or submaximal) exercise, and during maximal effort work. For example, you can measure an untrained individual's resting heart rate, train the person for several weeks or months, and then measure resting heart rate again to see what change has occurred. Resting heart rate declines with regular exercise, probably because of a combination of decreased sympathetic tone, increased parasympathetic tone, and decreased intrinsic firing rate of the sinoatrial node. Stroke volume at rest increases as a result of increased time for ventricular filling and an increased myocardial contractility. Little or no change occurs in cardiac output at rest, because the decline in heart rate is compensated for by the increase in stroke volume.

51. A. The purpose of the fitness assessment is to develop a proper exercise prescription (the data collected through appropriate fitness assessments assist the health/fitness specialist in developing safe, effective programs of exercise based on the individual client's current fitness status), to evaluate the rate of progress

(baseline and follow-up testing indicate progression toward fitness goals), and to motivate (fitness assessments provide information needed to develop reasonable, attainable goals). Progress toward or attainment of a goal is a strong motivator for continued participation in an exercise program.

52. C. Basic principles of care for musculoskeletal injuries include the objectives for care of exercise-related injuries, which are to decrease pain, reduce swelling, and prevent further injury. These objectives can be met in most cases by following "RICE" guidelines. RICE stands for "Rest, Ice, Compression, Elevation." Rest will prevent further injury and ensure that the healing process will begin. Ice is used to reduce swelling, bleeding, inflammation, and pain. Compression also helps to reduce swelling and bleeding. Compression is achieved by the use of elastic wraps or tape. Elevation helps to decrease the blood flow to and avoid excessive pressure on the injured area.

53. D. Various systems of resistance training exist that differ in their combinations of sets, repetitions, and resistance applied, all in an effort to overload the muscle. Circuit weight training uses a series of exercises performed in succession, with minimal rest between exercises. Various health benefits as well as modest improvements in aerobic capacity have been demonstrated as a result of circuit weight training. Super-sets refers to consecutive sets for antagonistic muscle groups with no rest between sets or multiple exercises for a specific muscle group with little or no rest. Split routines entail exercising different

body parts on different days or during different sessions. Pyramids are performed either in ascending (increasing the resistance within a set of repetitions or from one set to the next) or descending (decreasing the resistance within a set of repetitions or from one set to the next) fashion.

54. D. Large muscle group activity performed in rhythmic fashion over prolonged periods facilitates the greatest improvements in aerobic fitness. Walking, running, cycling, swimming, stair climbing, aerobic dance, rowing, and cross-country skiing are examples of these types of activities. Weight training should not be considered an appropriate activity for enhancing aerobic fitness, but should be part of a comprehensive exercise program to improve muscular strength and muscular endurance. The mode(s) of activity should be selected based on the principle of specificity—that is, with attention to the desired outcomes—and to maintain the participation and enjoyment of the individual.

55. C. The number of times per day or per week that a person exercises is interrelated with both the intensity and the duration of activity. Generally, sedentary persons or those with poor fitness may benefit from multiple short-duration, low-intensity exercise sessions per day. Individual goals, preferences, limitations, and time constraints also will determine frequency and the relationship between duration, frequency, and intensity.

The American
Council on
Exercise

CHAPTER 2

The American Council on Exercise (ACE) is a nonprofit organization that is committed to enriching people's quality of life through safe and effective exercise and physical activity. ACE's goal is to protect all segments of society against ineffective fitness products, programs, and trends through its ongoing public education, outreach, and research. ACE further seeks to protect the public by setting certification and continuing education standards for fitness professionals.

Founded in 1985, ACE is one of the largest global fitness certification, education, and training organizations, with more than 50,000 certified professionals worldwide. Given ACE's long experience in certification, education, and training, its programs are among the most respected in the fitness industry.

Tell Me about ACE's Philosophy

For the fitness professional, ACE is dedicated to providing unparalleled education, knowledge, and professional skills to guarantee career growth.

For the consumer, ACE is committed to serving the public as a qualified source for competent and experienced fitness professionals, and an established resource for comprehensive, unbiased, scientific research affecting today's fitness industry.

ACE is dedicated to keeping those seeking a career as a certified personal trainer at the forefront of the latest fitness trends and exercise science through knowledge of safe and effective exercise and physical activity. Just as important, all ACE-certified professionals are guided by the ACE's principles of professional conduct.

The ACE Code of Ethics states that ACE-certified professionals promise to

- Provide safe and effective instruction.
- Provide equal and fair treatment to all clients.
- Stay up-to-date on the latest health and fitness research and understand its practical application.
- Maintain current CPR certification and knowledge of first-aid services.
- Comply with all applicable business, employment, and intellectual property laws.
- Uphold and enhance public appreciation of and trust in the health and fitness industry.
- Maintain the confidentiality of all client information.
- Refer clients to more qualified health or medical professionals when appropriate.
- Establish and maintain clear professional boundaries.

ACE's mission to create a healthier world by developing and promoting safe and effective fitness practices and programs extends far beyond the fitness industry. ACE extends its industry expertise and unbiased perspective by providing a myriad of free health and fitness information to the general public and serves as an advising council and consumer steward for all things fitness.

ACE has also earned the reputation for being a consumer advocate and Workout Watchdog through university-based research and testing that targets fitness products and trends, and aims to protect the public from unqualified fitness professionals and unsafe and ineffective products, programs, and instruction.

ACE accomplishes its promotion of safe and effective exercise and physical activity, fitness products, programs, and trends through extensive research and studies in all areas of health and fitness, as well as public education regarding scientifically sound health and fitness practices. Since 1995, ACE has enlisted the expertise of top researchers at major universities across the country to conduct studies on fitness products and trends.

In 2009, ACE conducted a study on the perfect push-up and the benefits of boot-camp-style workouts; and in 2008, the organization commissioned a study on the pros and cons of the Wii Sports. ACE is currently researching the Wii Fit for a study that will be released later this year. These studies appear in ACE's bimonthly publication *Fitness Matters* and at www.acefitness.org/getfit/research.

Tell Me about ACE Certifications

The decision to pursue professional certification is an important first step in being recognized as a competent practitioner in one's discipline. ACE offers prospective candidates four accredited fitness certification programs—each with a full complement of study preparation materials—designed to accommodate a variety of learning styles and budgets.

Personal Trainer

Personal training is one of the fastest-growing professions in the health and fitness industry. The American Council on Exercise's acclaimed Personal Trainer Certification is designed for trainers providing any form of one-on-one or small-group fitness instruction.

Advanced Health and Fitness Specialist

This rewarding certification prepares the advanced professional to provide in-depth preventative and postrehabilitative fitness programming that addresses common diseases and disorders seen on a daily basis (e.g., cardiovascular disease, obesity, type 2 diabetes, and musculoskeletal ailments).

Group Fitness Instructor

The ACE Group Fitness Instructor certification is designed for fitness professionals teaching any form of exercise in a group setting, and demonstrates to class participants that the instructor has the foundation of knowledge and skills necessary to teach a safe and effective group fitness class, no matter what type of modality.

Lifestyle and Weight Management Consultant

The Lifestyle and Weight Management Consultant certification shows clients that their consultant has the knowledge to develop sound, balanced weight management programs that bring together the three critical components of long-term weight management success: nutrition, exercise, and lifestyle change.

Why Did ACE Pursue NCCA Accreditation of Its Certifications Programs?

Fitness professionals play an important role in health care by helping clients to improve their fitness and health through safe and effective exercise programs. The American Council on Exercise believes that in order to protect the public from harm caused by ineffective and unsafe exercise programs, fitness professionals should be held to the same level of professional competence as the other professionals working in allied health care.

In 1977, Congress created the National Commission for Health Certifying Agencies (NCHCA) to develop standards for quality certification in allied health fields and to accredit organizations that met those standards. In 1987, the NCHCA evolved into the National Organization for Competency Assurance (NOCA), a nonprofit, 501(c)(3) organization, to expand accreditation to certification programs outside of health care.

The National Commission for Certifying Agencies (NCCA) is the accrediting body of NOCA. The NCCA has rigorous standards that certification programs must meet in order to earn accreditation. Certification programs that meet all NCCA standards are awarded NCCA accreditation, which recognizes that the steps required to earn the certification adequately assess whether a candidate has the knowledge, skills, and ability required to work as a competent professional in a given field with minimum supervision.

The NCCA has reviewed and accredited many certification programs in allied health care, including the credentials for registered dietitians (RD), registered occupational therapists (OTR), athletic trainers (ATC), doctors of podiatric medicine (DPM), nurse practitioners (NP), registered nurses (RN), certified registered nurse anesthetists (CRNA), licensed massage therapists (LMT), and emergency medical technicians (EMT), as well as personal trainers, group fitness instructors, and advanced fitness professionals.

Each of these professional credentials has a unique set of eligibility requirements and specific steps for earning the credential, but they all have in common accreditation from the NCCA as the benchmark for validating that a professional holding the credential is qualified to provide safe and effective care and services to the public within the defined scope of practice.

The American Council on Exercise was one of the first organizations to understand the value of and pursue accreditation for its fitness certification programs. In 2003, ACE was granted accreditation by the NCCA for all four ACE certification programs (Personal Trainer, Advanced Health and Fitness Specialist, Group Fitness Instructor, and Lifestyle and Weight Management Consultant).

The initial impetus for earning accreditation from the NCCA stemmed from the 2002 recommendation from the Board of the International Health, Racquet, and Sportsclub Association (IHRSA), which stated:

> Whereas, given the increasing importance personal training plays in health, fitness and sports clubs, IHRSA recommends that, as of December 31, 2005, member clubs hire personal trainers who hold at least one current certification from a certifying organization/agency that has obtained third party accreditation of its certification procedures and protocols from an independent, experienced, and nationally recognized accrediting body. Furthermore, given the twenty-six year history of the National Organization for Competency Assurance (NOCA) in establishing quality standards for certifying agencies, IHRSA has identified the National Commission for Certifying Agen-

cies (NCCA), the accreditation body of NOCA, as being an acceptable accrediting organization.

In the fitness industry, NCCA accreditation has become recognized as the third-party standard for accreditation of certifications for personal trainers and other fitness professions, as seen in the following professional standards, guidelines, and recommendations:

The *Medical Fitness Association (MFA)*, the professional membership organization for medically integrated health and fitness facilities, has made it a standard that medical fitness facilities hire *only* fitness professionals who hold NCCA accredited certifications.

The *American College of Sports Medicine (ACSM) Health/Fitness Facility Standards and Guidelines* recommends that in meeting the Standards for Health/Fitness Facility Professional Staff and Independent Contractors, clubs hire only fitness directors, group exercise directors, fitness instructors (including personal trainers), and group exercise instructors who hold "certification from a nationally recognized and accredited certifying organization." It then states, "In this instance, the term *accredited* refers to certification programs that have received third-party approval of its certification procedures and practices from an appropriate agency, such as the National Commission for Certifying Agencies (NCCA)."

The *International Health, Racquet, and Sportsclub Association* recommends that club owners hire only personal trainers with certifications from agencies accredited by the NCCA or an equivalent accrediting organization.

There are other professional organizations that are currently in the process of developing voluntary fitness facility standards (e.g., NSF International) that will include requirements for hiring fitness professionals

▶ Certification Exam Tips

- Response options on the ACE exams are randomized. If you know absolutely nothing about a question, it is best to simply guess and move on.

- Pace yourself and make efficient use of your time. You should be halfway through the exam (or slightly more) when half of your time is up.

- Answer the easy questions first. More difficult questions can always be answered later.

- Read each question carefully and avoid skimming or speed reading. Be sure you understand what the question is asking. Underline key or bolded phrases: BEST, MOST, and so on.

- Try to anticipate what the answer is, but still read all the response options carefully before finalizing an answer. Remember that there is only one correct answer, and two response options may appear to be similar without careful reading.

- Don't overanalyze or read into the question. Each question is written as clearly as possible and should be interpreted as it appears. There is no hidden meaning or attempt to be tricky.

- Eliminate the least plausible response options. Eliminating one or two response options will increase your chances of selecting the correct answer with an educated guess.

- Take care in marking your answer sheet. Be sure that the question you are working on in your exam booklet corresponds to the mark you are making on your answer sheet.

- Answer every question. Remember, there is no penalty for guessing.

- Although first impressions are best, change your answer if you feel strongly about it.

that recognize the NCCA accreditation. In reference to the ACSM Health/Facility Standard and the IHRSA recommendation, the only other organization for possible consideration as a credible accreditation organization for certifying agencies is the American National Standards Institute (ANSI), which focuses primarily on third-party accreditation of industrial and workplace safety and quality standards.

The U.S. Department of Labor (DOL) Bureau of Labor Statistics reported in the 2008–2009 edition of its *Occupational Outlook Handbook* that most personal trainers *must* obtain certification in the fitness field to gain employment, explaining that there are many fitness organizations that offer certification and that "becoming certified by one of the top certification organizations is increasingly important, especially for personal trainers." The DOL then goes on to state, "One way to ensure that a certifying organization is reputable is to see that it is accredited by the National Commission for Certifying Agencies." The American Council on Exercise is one of the few organizations specifically identified by the DOL as offering high-quality, accredited certifications for personal trainers.

What Are the Benefits of Becoming ACE Certified?

ACE-certified professionals enjoy a number of exclusive benefits that include discounts on apparel, product, education, and liability insurance; participation in client training programs; and a free profile listing on "Find an ACE Trainer" (available to the public).

Understanding the need to provide ACE trainers with career opportunities, ACE teamed with the AARP as the provider of personal training services under a new fitness program for AARP members. Focused on prevention, this program provides information, resources, and services to help AARP's 39 million members lead active, healthier lifestyles.

This opportunity to expand their client base and income potential is available only to ACE-certified trainers who are enrolled in the program. In addition, ACE actively promotes the benefits of hiring an ACE trainer through more than 1.8 billion media impressions per year. Consumers are encouraged to visit www.acefitness.org to "Find an ACE Trainer."

To be in a position to affect national and state initiatives that promote more active lifestyles for all Americans, ACE is mobilizing its base of more than 50,000 professionals to work to pass laws that will help to effect societal changes leading to a more fit America. Through ACE's Legislative Action Center, ACE professionals can monitor legislative issues that affect them, voice their opinions, and speak to their elected officials on important issues. This initiative is focused on establishing and enhancing an influential, powerful, and unified political voice for the fitness industry while strengthening ACE's commitment to public outreach and increasing the number of ACE-certified fitness professionals who actively participate in grassroots advocacy.

In addition to improving the professional standards of the fitness industry, ACE is committed to the health and well-being of the public and encourages all segments of society to enjoy the benefits of exercise. As the country's leading authority on fitness, ACE serves the public as an established resource for comprehensive, unbiased, scientific research affecting today's fitness industry, and disseminates this information, free of charge, via www.acefitness.org.

Free Health and Fitness Resources

Providing free health and fitness resources has helped ACE promote the benefits of physical activity and protect consumers against unsafe and ineffective fitness products and instruction. Through the Web page www.acefitness.org/GetFit, ACE publishes university-based exercise science research, an online exercise library, one-page Fit Facts on a variety of topics, healthy recipes, and other fitness tips at no cost to the general public.

ACE Fit Facts are concise, one-page health and fitness information sheets, each covering a different health or fitness subject. More than 100 topics are available. Each Fit Fact contains valuable how-to information and tips that range from advice on the best type of exercise for weight loss to exercising with health challenges to pointers on choosing a personal trainer.

Recently updated, ACE's exercise library features 130 exercises designed to target specific body parts, including the most sought-after abdominal, lower body, upper body, and core exercises. Recognizing that proper form is essential for any workout program, exercises were developed for all experience levels—beginner, intermediate, and advanced—with step-by-step details and accompanying photos that can be viewed in print or in motion. The search feature also allows users to select specific exercises based upon the equipment they have available.

The American Council on Exercise is dedicated to promoting the benefits of physical activity and protecting consumers against unsafe and ineffective health and fitness products, programs, and trends. ACE accomplishes this through ongoing extensive research and studies in all areas of health and fitness, as well as public education regarding scientifically sound health and fitness practices. Dubbed the "workout watchdog" by the *Wall Street Journal*, ACE has established a reputation as a consumer advocate. Since 1995, ACE has enlisted the expertise of top researchers at major universities across the country to conduct studies on fitness products and trends.

ACE Partnerships

ACE has collaborated with many organizations to help promote the benefits of fitness and to get the message out about the importance of living an active lifestyle. A few of these organizations are

- *AARP.* The AARP is the leading nonprofit, nonpartisan membership organization for people age 50 and over in the United States. Having a shared mission, both ACE and AARP were interested in providing a service to a population that has been greatly underserved by the fitness industry and whose members the means, motivation, and desire to enhance their quality of life through physical activity. ACE teamed with AARP as the provider of personal training services for AARP members. Focused on prevention, the ACE Trainer Program for AARP members provides information, resources, and discounted services—including access to health clubs and personal training—to help AARP members lead active, healthier lifestyles. Anyone interested in this program can visit www.acefitness.org/aarp for more information.
- *American Heart Association (AHA).* The American Council on Exercise partnered with the American Heart Association to enable fitness professionals to create a safer fitness environment and teach the invaluable skills of saving a life through AHA's CPR and AED programs.

  Additionally, ACE partnered with the American Heart Association to develop walking plans for people at various ability levels who want a physical activity routine. The AHA's Start! Walking program promotes walking as an activity because it's accessible, it's free, and it has the lowest dropout rate of any type of exercise. The free downloadable plans and a list of walking paths in various cities are available at www.startwalkingnow.org.

- *International Association of Fire Fighters (IAFF).* In support of ACE's mission and to help improve the safety, performance, and quality of life of uniformed personnel in the fire service industry, the American Council on Exercise, the International Association of Fire Fighters (IAFF), and the International Association of Fire Chiefs (IAFC) teamed to develop the Peer Fitness Trainer certification (PFT).

  Available throughout the United States and Canada, the PFT specialty certification prepares firefighters to design and implement fitness programs, improve the wellness and fitness of their departments, and assist with the physical training of recruits within their extreme work environment.

- *International Council on Active Aging (ICAA).* The ICAA's mission is to connect a community of like-minded professionals who share the goals of changing society's perceptions of aging and improving the quality of life for aging baby boomers and older adults. Working with the ICAA, ACE offers accredited fitness certifications and continuing education to staff members of wellness centers and senior living facilities. This helps to ensure that these professionals have the proper training, credentials, and knowledge to provide safe and effective exercise programs to the 50+ population. Of key interest is ACE's Advanced Health and Fitness Specialist certification, which focuses on preventative and postrehabilitative fitness programming that addresses cardiovascular disease, obesity, type 2 diabetes, musculoskeletal ailments, and other disorders commonly found in older adults.

- *Youth fitness.* With childhood obesity on the rise, the American Council on Exercise is dedicated to improving youth health and fitness. ACE provides educational materials to those who are working to promote youth fitness: educators, fitness professionals, health professionals, and parents. ACE-certified professionals created "Operation FitKids," a free curriculum designed for educators looking to integrate health and fitness into classroom learning. This program was developed for grades three to five to teach kids the importance of a healthy and active lifestyle. The program is available in an easy-to-download PDF format at www.acefitness.org.

What Study and Continuing Education Programs Does ACE Offer?

With candidates coming from a broad range of backgrounds, the importance of planning a *study strategy* is undeniable. In addition to a variety of home study kits and online, live, and Webinar-based exam review programs, ACE introduced the Study Coach Program. This unique service offers free 12- and 20-week study plans that outline the essential points and key concepts required to focus studies. To assist in tailoring a study program to an individual's learning style; ACE provides an interactive tool to identify the right combination of materials based on the candidate's professional background, education, and experience.

ACE Study Materials

ACE offers manuals, workbooks, sample tests, online exam review courses, Webinar courses, and a variety of other study materials for each

ACE certification program. For a complete listing of ACE study materials, visit the ACE Web site (www.acefitness.org) or call the ACE Educational Services Department at (888) 825-3636.

ACE Certification Candidate Handbook

To assist candidates in preparing to become ACE-certified professionals, ACE offers a complementary certification candidate handbook that can be downloaded as a PDF document from the following Web site: www.ace fitness.org/getcertified/pdfs/Certification-Exam-Candidate-Handbook.pdf. This handbook provides candidates with detailed information about ACE certifications, including

- ACE Professional Standards and Certification Accreditation
- ACE Code of Ethics
- ACE Professional Practices and Disciplinary Procedures
- ACE Certification Programs and Eligibility
- Exam content outlines
- Exam formats and test-taking strategies
- Study resources
- Exam registration, fees, administration, scoring, and results
- Pass rates for ACE exams
- International exam administration
- Exam development procedures
- Maintaining your ACE certification
- Continuing education policies
- Career development
- Protection of privacy, confidentiality, security, and records retention

Continuing Education

ACE's Continuing Education Center provides more than 2,000 continuing education courses and events covering in-demand topics such as exercise science, special populations and postrehab, strength training, nutrition, youth fitness, and sports performance, among others. Programs are available to current and prospective certified professionals, and provide the training needed to design and implement safe and effective exercise programs, enhance professional skills, and maintain credentials. ACE continuing education courses, practical training workshops, and symposiums are staffed with leading fitness educators throughout the world and are offered in a variety of formats to meet the ever-changing needs of today's students.

As a partner throughout an individual's career, ACE recognizes the importance of professional growth and the need for easy-to-use and effective professional, business, and educational resources and tools. Via the ACE Pro Site, trainers have free access to hundreds of business templates such as a financial plan, billing agreement, cancellation policy, sales letters, and other such documents. The career planning tools and marketing resources offer guidance on how to do everything from writing a résumé and announcing new credentials to running a successful fitness business. Plus, trainers have access to a personal reference desk through SPORT-Discus that boasts a library of more than 1,500 industry journals, articles, and text to address even the most experienced trainer's questions.

Tell Me about the ACE Certification Examinations

ACE certification exams assess a candidate's ability to make safe and effective decisions regarding health history and risk factor information, fitness assessments, exercise programming and progressions, rapport, motivation and program adherence, professional responsibilities, scope of practice, and other topics specific to each certification.

Each ACE certification exam comprises 150 multiple-choice questions, with the ACE Personal Trainer Certification exam also including a second exam component consisting of client scenarios that require candidates to select the responses that are most appropriate, given the client's reported health, fitness, current program, and other personal factors such as family or work commitments.

For the ACE Personal Trainer certification exam, the multiple-choice exam makes up 75 percent of the final score, while the client scenario exam makes up the remaining 25 percent of the final score. For all other ACE certification programs, the multiple-choice questions make up the complete exam.

ACE employs CASTLE Worldwide, Inc., a professional testing company, to manage the development, delivery, and scoring of ACE certification exams and to ensure that ACE certifications adhere to national testing standards. ACE assembles committees of working fitness professionals who have been identified as subject matter experts to write, review, and validate questions for ACE certification exams. The knowledge, skills, and abilities tested by the multiple-choice questions on an ACE certification exam must follow the exam content outline for the specific ACE certification program.

Each question written is referenced to a specific area of the content outline for the specific exam, and also has a reference to an appropriate resource that includes ACE study materials and current industry standards, guidelines, and position papers (e.g., those of the American Medical Association, American Heart Association, American College of Sports Medicine, American College of Obstetricians and Gynecologists, or U.S. Department of Agriculture). Each multiple-choice question is reviewed by at least three subject matter experts to ensure that the question is appropriate, the correct response is in fact correct, and the incorrect answers are in fact incorrect.

Three types of multiple-choice questions are used on the ACE certification exams: recall, application, and analysis. Application and analysis questions make up the majority of the questions (70 to 85 percent) on ACE multiple-choice exams. These questions assess the candidates' ability to solve problems and apply their working knowledge in circumstances that they can expect to experience in the field. The remaining questions on an ACE multiple-choice exam will be recall questions, which are cognitive in nature and test only the candidate's ability to recall knowledge.

The information that follows is designed to give ACE certification exam candidates a better understanding of multiple-choice question design and the difference between recall, application, and analysis questions.

Anatomy of a Multiple-Choice Question

A multiple-choice question consists of a stem and response options. The stem is a statement or a question and often includes key words to help the candidate understand what is being asked or assessed. The stem may be presented as a direct question, an incomplete statement, or a best answer format. For instance:

Direct: What muscle flexes the elbow joint?
Incomplete statement: The muscle that flexes the elbow joint is
Best answer format: Which exercise MOST effectively strengthens the flexors of the elbow joint?

Response options consist of one correct or clearly best answer and several distracters (all of which are incorrect). Distractors usually contain common errors and are often drawn from the same conceptual category as the correct response. Distractors are also similar to the correct response in length, complexity, grammatical construction, and so on. For example:

Which of the following muscles causes lateral flexion of the spine?

A. Latissimus dorsi
B. Rhomboid major
C. Quadratus lumborum
D. Transverse abdominis
(The correct answer is C.)

Test-Taking Strategies for ACE Certification Exams

High-quality hands-on experience is probably one of the strongest predictors for passing the ACE certification exams, perhaps because of the number of application and analysis questions. Those who lack experience in designing exercise programs or leading exercise in a group setting may be at a disadvantage. If candidates are presented with a question that assesses an area in which they have no experience, they have only their opinions or biases available to help them choose response options.

As mentioned, all exam questions have only one correct answer and three plausible distractors. Candidates with more experience are better able to determine the plausibility of all the response options (in other words, to see through the smoke) and recognize the correct answer with little difficulty. Those who lack experience may be left to guess, and when two or three response options appear to be equally plausible, they may find the question somewhat tricky.

Specific exam preparation is also critical. All exam questions are based on an exam content outline (found in the appendix of each respective ACE manual). The exam content outline lists the specific knowledge base upon which questions are written. Each exam content outline is derived from a formal role delineation study (job analysis) for personal trainers, group fitness instructors, lifestyle and weight management consultants, and advanced health and fitness specialists. As with the principle of specificity of exercise training, candidates are better served if they guide their study based on these knowledge statements. This way, candidates can determine their deficiencies in theory or practical experience.

Familiarity with the exam content outline can also help alleviate test anxiety. Candidates who are unfamiliar with the exam content outline may have the misconception that the ACE exams are anatomy- and physiology-based or that only the information presented in the ACE manuals will be assessed.

Though the ACE manuals for personal trainers, group fitness instructors, lifestyle and weight management consultants, and advanced health and fitness specialists are widely respected, keep in mind that they should be considered helpful resources, rather than the sole authority. Candidates do themselves and the industry a disservice if they believe that studying an ACE manual alone is a comprehensive resource for their fitness knowledge.

ACE Sample Questions

(Answers can be found at the end of the chapter.)

Recall Questions

Recall questions assess the candidate's knowledge of facts and terminology, and their comprehension of important principles. Candidates are asked to demonstrate their ability to recall learned information. A relatively small number of recall questions are presented on the ACE exams, since they assess the lowest cognition level.

For example:

1. Which muscle flexes the elbow joint?

   A. Biceps brachii
   B. Triceps brachii
   C. Biceps femoris
   D. Triceps surae

Application Questions

An application question poses a problem or situation that the candidate would be likely to encounter while working in the profession. Application questions assess the candidate's ability to recognize the proper use of factual information and principles in solving problems that fitness professionals might experience on the job.

The following question refers to the information given here for Sarah, a new female client:

Age:	27 years
Height:	5 ft. 4 in. (162.5 cm)
Weight:	125 lb. (56.7 kg)
Lean body mass:	90 lb. (40.8 kg)
Triceps skinfold:	16 mm
Suprailium skinfold:	25 mm

2. What is Sarah's body-fat percentage?

A. 23 percent

B. 28 percent

C. 33 percent

D. 38 percent

3. A client who has limited range of motion in hip flexion would **MOST** likely have tightness in which of the following muscles?

A. Gluteus minimus

B. Rectus femoris

C. Tensor fasciae latae

D. Biceps femoris

Analysis Questions

Analysis questions assess the candidate's ability to examine information and understand the relationship between its components. In other words, how do the parts work together to make a whole? In this manner, by correctly analyzing the facts, a candidate can properly identify a problem and its appropriate solution.

For example:

The food label on a 12-ounce bag of candy provides the following information:

Serving size: 6 pieces (40 g)
Servings per container: 8
Amount per serving:
    Calories: 160
    Calories from fat: 27
% Daily Value:
    Total fat: 3 g (4 percent)
    Saturated fat: 0.5 g (3 percent)
    Sugars: 30 g (11 percent)
    Protein: less than 1 g (trace)

4. What is the total amount and percentage of calories that come from fat in the entire bag?

    A. 27 calories, 4 percent
    B. 216 calories, 17 percent
    C. 27 calories, 17 percent
    D. 252 calories, 20 percent

Client Scenario Exam

The client scenario portion of the exam applies only to the ACE Personal Trainer certification exam. The purpose of the client scenarios is to test the candidate's decision-making ability. The client scenarios are designed to simulate, as closely as possible, the types of clientele and situations that an actual certified personal trainer may encounter in a professional setting.

Written Simulation Exam

The written simulation exam applies only to the Personal Trainer certification exam. The purpose of the ACE Personal Trainer written simulation exam is to test the candidate's decision-making ability. The written simulation exam consists of two client scenarios, designed to simulate, as closely as possible, the types of situations that an actual certified personal trainer may encounter in a professional setting.

The written simulation exam consists of two booklets that the candidate receives: a problem booklet and an answer booklet.

Problem Booklet

- The problem booklet contains two problems, or client scenarios.
- Each problem begins with an introduction that provides information about the client.
- Each problem is divided into sections (approximately four to eight sections per problem).
- Each section begins with an introduction/scenario that describes a set of circumstances.
- Each section also contains a list of questions/actions/decisions from which the candidate chooses those that he or she deems to be most appropriate given the circumstances at that time.

ACE Sample Test Answers

Recall Question

1. A. Biceps brachii

Application Questions

1. B. 28 percent

2. D. Biceps femoris

Analysis Questions

1. B. 216 calories, 17 percent

CHAPTER 3

The National Council on Strength and Fitness

The National Council on Strength and Fitness (NCSF) is a member-driven organization and board for certification providing support services, educational programs, public outreach, and professional credentialing for the personal training profession. As a leading authority in the health and fitness industry, the mission of the NCSF is to serve the interests of both the personal training profession and the general public.

Tell Me about the NCSF and Its Philosophy

The mission of the National Council on Strength and Fitness is to provide students with advanced scholarship that embodies the principles of lifetime health and fitness. Through visionary leadership and academic integrity, the organization is devoted to empowering students with the knowledge and skills needed to deliver unsurpassed professional practices within the health and fitness profession.

The NCSF Certified Personal Trainer credential is the premier certification afforded to those who have the aptitude and willingness to master the disciplines of health, exercise, and nutritional science. The NCSF education programs develop qualified fitness professionals, sound in both theory and practice. The NCSF excels in professional academics by emphasizing the needs of the learner, the needs of the employers, and the needs of the general consumer.

The NCSF Board for Certification maintains a certification program that is in complete compliance with all applicable standards of test development and administration. The NCSF Board for Certification is made up of elected officials from the fitness industry, the medical community, and experts from academia that demand valid testing procedures, reliable testing measures, and the best testing environment for certification candidates.

The NCSF Board for Certification serves as the credentialing body for the organization and regulates the professional practices of certified personal trainers. This national board is the authority over the Personal Trainer certification program, providing a legally defensible Personal Trainer certification to individuals who successfully pass the NCSF board exam.

The NCSF works cooperatively with other allied health licensing and certification boards to provide continuing education and network support for the following professions: licensed physical therapists and physical therapy assistants, registered dietitians and registered dietitian technicians, and certified athletic trainers.

What about Accreditation?

The NCSF Certified Personal Trainer credential has been reviewed by and received accreditation from the National Commission for Certifying Agencies (NCCA), the accrediting board for the National Organization for Competency Assurance (NOCA).

Describe the Exam Preparation Process

The NCSF offers several different educational models and a variety of materials to help you prepare for your NCSF Certified Personal Trainer examination. Here is a discussion of the program options.

Workshop Course Intended Audience

The Certified Personal Trainer Workshop Course is designed specifically for students who prefer self-paced, directed study combined with a two-day, hands-on learning-by-doing component that complements the learning experience. This format allows you the opportunity to review the exam content areas while turning theoretical concepts into the practical applications required of a personal trainer. This program covers the same content areas as both the home study course and the Personal Trainer School.

Home Study Course Intended Audience

Offering the flexibility of self-paced learning in the convenience of your home, the NCSF Personal Trainer Home Study Course effectively covers the topics necessary to successfully pass the NCSF Certified Personal Trainer exam in a format that fits into a busy schedule. Modeled after a college correspondence course, the home study course uses a systematic approach to teach you the science behind sound fitness training and exercise programming. This program covers the same content areas as both the workshop and the Personal Trainer School course.

Personal Trainer School Intended Audience

The NCSF Personal Trainer School is a structured 32-contact-hour program designed for students who are seeking maximal supervision in a classroom-based environment. Each class addresses key content areas from the Certified Personal Trainer exam, as well as pertinent topics necessary to ensure your development as a qualified professional. This program covers the same content areas as both the home study and workshop courses.

Individual Exam Preparation Materials

Individual personal trainer exam preparation materials are available for candidates preparing for the NCSF Personal Trainer certification exam. Current certified personal trainers may also obtain additional professional reference materials to aid them in their personal trainer practice. The personal trainer exam preparation materials provide exam candidates with the option of preparing for the NCSF Certified Personal Trainer exam in a noncourse format. Simply choose the resources that best serve your learning needs, and your materials will be immediately shipped to you.

Tell Me about the Personal Trainer Certification Exam

The Board for Certification testing service has used input from more than 20,000 surveys of facility owners, fitness managers, experts from academia, health professionals, and practicing personal trainers to develop its Personal Trainer certification. The result is a true measure of professional qualification and subsequent valid and reliable exams that hold up under legal scrutiny.

The National Council on Strength and Fitness offers its Personal Trainer certification exam through Prometric testing centers. With more than 400 testing locations throughout North America and convenient 24-hour examination scheduling, Prometric is the leading worldwide provider of comprehensive, technology-based testing and assessment services. This provides exam candidates with full access to the latest testing technology, award-winning customer service, and flexible exam scheduling.

The NCSF ensures that each candidate has all the necessary information required to register, schedule, and sit for her certification examination. Once the candidate has scheduled her exam, she simply attends her confirmed appointment.

The certification exam is a 150-question multiple-choice examination. Each candidate will have three hours to complete the exam. The NCSF examination is computer-based, and each candidate will receive a full tutorial regarding the use of the exam equipment prior to the start. Technical assistance will also be provided during the examination itself if any problems should arise.

Candidates will receive sectional analysis as well as overall exam scoring upon completion of the certification exam. The cut score for successful exam completion is 62 percent.

What about Exam Content?

The Personal Trainer certification identifies individuals who are qualified to prescribe and instruct exercise for healthy individuals or those with controlled disease based on evaluative criteria.

Eligible certification candidates must meet the minimum passing score to attain certification. The 150 questions on the certification examination are designed to assess the requisite nine (9) content areas. The specific number of test items for each content area has been determined by a job task analysis.

The exam is broken down as follows:

Functional anatomy	12.90%
Exercise physiology	8.90%
Health and physical fitness	10.50%
Screening and evaluation	12.10%
Nutrition	10.50%
Weight management	8.10%
Exercise prescription and programming considerations	14.50%
Training instruction	17.70%
Considerations for special populations	4.80%

What about Continuing Education and Credential Maintenance?

Recertification is an integral part of a board certification program. The decision to maintain a credential is equally as important as the decision to become certified in the first place.

Recertification can be accomplished in two ways through the NCSF Board for Certification: (1) participating in continued education course work and qualifying activities to earn the required continued education units (CEUs), or (2) retaking the certification exam.

To retake the exam, a candidate simply submits an application for eligibility, pays the registration fee, and is retested in accordance with the exam administration policies. To recertify using continued education, a certified professional needs to accumulate 10 continued education units/credits over the certification term. This can be accomplished through any of the qualifying criteria listed here. The CEUs must be completed prior to the expiration date of the certification.

The NCSF Board for Certification Recertification Standards for Practice Committee determined the term for certification to be two years. The rationale for the recertification interval is fourfold:

1. Because of the relative infancy of the profession and the rate at which new practices and theories are being identified and implemented within the profession, the period of time for recertification must reflect a duration that will provide for adequate updates in knowledge.

2. The number of contact hours required for a four-year term is set at 40 hours. This number was determined by a survey of other board recertification requirements for similar professions and based on committee findings and determinations. To comply with rationale 1, the contact hours had to be split in half to produce a fair representation of the term-to-contact-hour ratio—essentially a requirement of 10 contact hours per year.

3. The term had to be long enough to allow the certified professionals to earn the appropriate credits, but short enough to keep the certified professionals motivated to engage in education and training.

4. The determination was also based on recommendations to initiate a step toward best practice that would require routine annual continued education participation in attempts to help

certified professionals avoid long periods of education inactivity and reduce certification attrition rates.

Category	Maximum Value from Category
A. NCSF CEU library	10 units
B. NCSF approved courses and programs	10 units
C. NCSF article quizzes	10 units
D. NCSF exam preparation courses	7 units
E. NCSF ethics	3 units
F. College courses	10 units
G. Nonapproved courses and programs	6 units
H. Personal development	5 units
I. CPR/first aid/AED	2 units

NCSF Sample Test Questions and Answers

Functional Anatomy

Relative percentage of certification exam: 12.9%

1. Which of the following examples would present the longest resistance arm, making it the most mechanically disadvantaged position for the body during resistance training?
   A. Side dumbbell raises at 90° of shoulder abduction
   B. Dumbbell fly on a flat bench at the end range of motion (full horizontal adduction)

C. Biceps curl at 90° of elbow flexion

D. Starting position of triceps pushdown

2. Which of these muscles is part of the rotator cuff?

   A. Coracobrachialis

   B. Teres major

   C. Supraspinatus

   D. Pectoralis minor

Exercise Physiology

Relative percentage of certification exam: 8.9%

3. Which of the following training techniques is most likely
   to cause the greatest caloric expenditure from excess postexercise oxygen consumption (EPOC) following a one-hour
   exercise bout?

   A. Weight training using 60–75% 1RM

   B. Yoga

   C. Steady-state aerobic training in the fat-burning zone

   D. Interval aerobic training in the carbohydrate zone

4. Completing three minutes of moderate-intensity exercise would
   use fuel primarily from which metabolic pathway?

   A. Aerobic metabolism of proteins

   B. Anaerobic metabolism of creatine phosphate

C. Aerobic metabolism of lipids

D. Anaerobic metabolism of carbohydrates

Health and Physical Fitness

Relative percentage of certification exam: 10.5%

5. Which of the following is NOT a direct cause of atherosclerosis?

A. Hypertension

B. Smoking

C. High LDL cholesterol

D. High-carbohydrate diet

6. Your client had the following screening results:

44-year-old male	HDL cholesterol: 37 mg/dl
RHR: 86 bpm	Body fat percentage: 28%
RBP: 132/90 mmHg	VO_2 max: 32 ml/kg/min
Total cholesterol: 217 mg/dl	Failed Apley shoulder screen (both arms)

Following eight weeks of training, his VO_2 max increased to 38 ml/kg/min. Assuming that all other factors in his life remained the same, which of the responses below would most likely accompany the aerobic efficiency change?

A. RHR 78 bpm, RBP 130/85, HDL 46 mg/dl, body fat 26%

B. RHR 86 bpm, RBP 129/94, HDL 35 mg/dl, body fat 25%

C. RHR 70 bpm, RBP 122/81, HDL 30 mg/dl, body fat 20%

D. Total cholesterol 200 mg/dl, HDL 40 mg/dl, body fat 18%

Screening and Evaluation

Relative percentage of certification exam: 12.1%

7. When using correct skinfold measurements to evaluate body fat, the standard estimation of error is approximately _____% when an experienced tester performs the assessment.

    A. 1–2%

    B. 3–4%

    C. 5–6%

    D. skinfold assessment value does not have a standard error

8. Bronchodilators are sometimes used as medication for asthmatics. If during the screening it is identified that a person routinely takes these medications, how will the medication influence the exercise prescription?

    A. It will have little or no effect.

    B. It will require decreased heart rate intensities during exercise.

    C. It will require longer rest periods.

    D. It will require lower intensities applied for longer duration.

Nutrition

Relative percentage of certification exam: 10.5%

9. Which of the following vitamins is a water-soluble antioxidant?

    A. Vitamin C
    B. Vitamin A
    C. Vitamin E
    D. Vitamin K

10. Based on nutritional guidelines, which would be an acceptable protein intake for a person who is physically active?

    A. 1.1 grams per kilogram of body weight
    B. 40% of total caloric intake
    C. 2.0 grams per kilogram of body weight
    D. 1.0 gram per pound

Weight Management

Relative percentage of certification exam: 8.1%

11. Weight loss measured immediately following exercise is mostly attributed to

    A. lipid metabolism.
    B. the breakdown of muscle protein.
    C. the loss of water.
    D. elevated levels of anabolic hormone.

12. Which of the following procedures measures subcutaneous fat to calculate body mass density for the prediction of body fatness?

   A. Body mass index
   B. Hydrostatic weighing
   C. Bioelectrical impedance
   D. Skinfold assessment

Exercise Prescription and Programming Considerations

Relative percentage of certification exam: 14.5%

13. Which of the following upper body resistance exercises would be inappropriate for a client who fails both the shoulder flexion and shoulder abduction flexibility screens?

   A. Overhead shoulder press
   B. One arm row
   C. Triceps kickback
   D. Push-ups

14. _____ refers to the amount of time between training bouts and is important to program appropriately so that adaptation responses are possible.
   A. Rest interval
   B. Recovery period
   C. Training volume
   D. Exercise duration

Training Instruction

Relative percentage of certification exam: 17.7%

15. During the execution of an abdominal curl-up exercise, the client should

   A. draw in the umbilicus and perform a posterior pelvic tilt to properly execute abdominal flexion.
   B. exhale while performing an anterior pelvic tilt.
   C. hold his or her breath to increase intra-abdominal pressure and release it at the top of the concentric phase.
   D. maintain a neutral spine throughout the movement.

16. Which of the following muscles, if tight, can affect pelvic positioning and lead to low back pain?

   A. Psoas major
   B. Vastus medialis
   C. Vastus lateralis
   D. Gastrocnemius

Considerations for Special Populations

Relative percentage of certification exam: 4.8%

17. The degenerative loss of muscle mass and strength usually attributed to disease or aging is termed

A. hypertrophy.

B. regeneration.

C. denervation.

D. sarcopenia.

18. Amenorrhea, osteoporosis, and anorexia nervosa are symptoms that are often seen in which of the population segments listed?

A. Females with severe obesity

B. Female athletes

C. Females over age 40

D. Individuals with fibromyalgia

Answers: Functional Anatomy

1. A. The further the resistance is from the body, the longer the resistance arm. The side dumbbell raise utilizes an extended arm abducted from the body and therefore creates a long resistance arm with a short lever arm. This reduces the mechanical advantage and increases the difficulty of the movement. The triceps pushdown and biceps curl use a resistance arm that is, at its greatest length, approximately half the distance of the full arm length. Although the straight arm fly also uses an extended arm, when the resistance is over the body, the resistance arm is controlled by mechanical advantage because gravity is directed into the joint rather than across it.

2. C. One of the four rotator cuff muscles, the supraspinatus is primarily responsible for humeral abduction to 30°. The other muscles of the rotator cuff are the infraspinatus, teres minor, and subscapularis. The infraspinatus and teres minor perform external humeral rotation, and the subscapularis is an internal humeral rotator. Though these muscles contribute to shoulder movements, a primary role of the rotator cuff is to stabilize and control the humeral head position in the articulating surface of the glenoid fossa.

Answers: Exercise Physiology

3. D. EPOC is commonly associated with a level of physiological disruption related to intensity and duration. Interval training allows the body to reach intensity levels that it cannot sustain

for prolonged periods of time. This training technique uses a combination of anaerobic and aerobic metabolisms to reach higher intensities (carbohydrate is the primary fuel), consequently causing an increase in oxygen demand. When the oxygen demand exceeds the amount available, oxygen debt occurs. Steady-state training in the "fat-burning zone" causes very little oxygen demand above what the body can deliver, limiting the metabolic disruption because the tissue is not heavily taxed. Supply generally equals demand, so postexercise debt is very limited. Although weight training can have a marked effect on EPOC when performed at high intensities with short rest intervals, low to moderate intensities with normal rest intervals do not have as dramatic an effect. Repetition ranges of 10–20 or 60–75% 1RM are often performed at higher intensities than steady-state training, and the oxygen demand exceeds 100 percent VO_2 max, but the longer rest periods commonly used in traditional weight training allow for nearly complete recovery. The very nature of interval aerobic training limits rest opportunities. Yoga may cause a very limited oxygen debt, but the nature of the activity and the measured MET levels of traditional yoga are such that the oxygen demand of the tissue is minimal. The caloric demands of traditional yoga classes are often limited compared to those of other forms of exercise.

4. D. The energy pathway primarily responsible for the first five minutes of sustained activity is called glycolysis, which refers to the breakdown of glucose, or sugar (carbohydrates). Glucose is stored as glycogen in both the skeletal muscle and the liver. The first few seconds of activity primarily use ATP, while the next

five to ten seconds use mostly the creatine phosphate system. Once sustained activity progresses beyond five minutes, aerobic metabolism takes over as the primary producer of energy. It takes approximately ten minutes before the body begins to utilize lipids for its energy needs.

Answers: Health and Physical Fitness

5. D. High-carbohydrate diets do not directly cause atherosclerosis or vessel blockage. However, the combined effects of refined carbohydrates, a sedentary lifestyle, and a diet high in fat have been linked to elevated triglycerides and increased risk for heart disease; smoking, hypertension, and high LDL cholesterol are all directly linked to the formation of plaque in the arteries.

6. A. If an exercise prescription increases a client's VO_2 max, other concurrent adaptations to improved cardiovascular health would typically include a lower resting heart rate, lower resting blood pressure, and increased HDL cholesterol, all of which are typically seen with increased cardiovascular fitness and aerobic training. In eight weeks, conservative changes take place, but over an extended period of time, more dramatic changes can occur. In some cases, genetics can limit some categorical improvements, but overall health is certainly improved.

Answers: Screening and Evaluation

7. B. Clinical data from criterion measures using hydrostatic weighing suggest that skinfold estimation of error is approximately

3.5%. Even experienced testers have a standard estimation of error of 3–4% when performing skinfold assessments. Prediction error can further increase with inappropriate regression equation selection. In most cases, skinfold testing is most accurate in relatively lean populations. Obese individuals have large folds that can increase measurement error rather significantly; obese individuals should be tested using girth assessments.

8. A. Bronchodilators are a class of drugs that help limit or prevent bronchospasm. They have no effect on resting or exercise heart rate or blood pressure and will improve exercise capacity to that of nonsymptomatic populations. Therefore, no change in the exercise prescription is necessary when someone is taking bronchodilators or uses an inhaler.

Answers: Nutrition

9. A. Vitamin C is a water-soluble antioxidant that neutralizes free radicals in aqueous environments. Beta carotene (the precursor for vitamin A) and vitamin E are lipid-soluble antioxidant vitamins. The general recommendation for vitamin C is 75–90 mg daily with a tolerable upper limit of 2,000 mg. Unused vitamin C is excreted in urine as a result of its water-soluble properties.

10. A. Based on nutritional guidelines, 1–1.2 grams of protein per kilogram of body weight would be an acceptable protein intake for proper nitrogen balance in a person who is physically active. An excessive protein intake can lead to toxicity and damage vital organs. For sedentary persons, 0.8–0.9 gram per

kilogram of body weight is recommended. Generally, 2.0 grams per kilogram of body weight is the accepted tolerable upper limit for strength athletes.

Answers: Weight Management

11. C. Weight loss immediately following exercise is attributed to water loss from temperature regulation and metabolic processes. To help regulate temperature during activity, the body releases fluid through the skin's sweat glands so that it can evaporate, releasing heat and cooling the body. Increased respiration also causes an increased loss of fluid to the air. Normally, respiration-related fluid loss accounts for about 300 ml per day. During activity involving elevated heart rates for sustained periods of time, that number can be increased to up to 5 ml per minute.

12. D. Skinfold assessment is used to measure the millimeter thickness of subcutaneous fat deposits in selected regions related to genetic fat patterning in men and women. The calculation of body density is based on the fact that 50–70% of normal fat storage occurs between the dermal layer of skin and muscle (subcutaneous). Depending on the protocol being used, different sites for the skinfold assessment exist for men and women because of gender-specific storage patterns.

Answers: Exercise Prescription

13. A. Deficiencies in ROM as identified by the shoulder flexion and abduction screens would suggest that tightness in the latis-

simus dorsi exists, since the lats serve to extend and adduct the shoulder. Therefore, proper performance of the overhead shoulder press would not be attainable. The press exercise requires the arm to be extended over the shoulder through the frontal plane (arm abduction), which, in this case, would be limited by tightness in the latissimus dorsi. Therefore, flexibility programming for the latissimus dorsi should be targeted for functional ROM prior to programming the overhead shoulder press, and an exercise such as side raises should be used for strengthening in the meantime.

14. B. The recovery period refers to the amount of time between exercise bouts. Recovery allows for the necessary replenishment of energy sources and for cellular adaptations to occur. Rest interval refers to the amount of time taken between exercise sets. Training volume refers to the total amount of work completed during a training bout. Training volume is calculated by multiplying the total number of sets and repetitions performed and loads lifted. Duration refers to the amount of time the actual exercise is being performed. In a typical one-hour resistance training program, the duration of work may only be 15–20 minutes.

Answers: Training Instruction

15. A. To reduce involvement of the hip flexors and prevent low back injury during trunk flexion while encouraging proper engagement of the transverse abdominis (TVA) and rectus abdominis, one should draw in the umbilicus before perform-

ing the posterior pelvic tilt during the execution of the abdominal curl-up exercise.

16. A. The psoas major is one of the primary hip flexors. When they are tight, the hip flexors pull on the pelvis and cause an anterior pelvic tilt, which can ultimately lead to the development of low back pain. The vastus lateralis and vastus medialis are two of the four muscles that make up the quadriceps and only cross the knee joint (responsible for knee extension). The gastrocnemius is a primary plantar flexor found in the lower leg.

Answers: Considerations for Special Populations

17. D. Sarcopenia is the loss of muscle mass associated with increasing age. In many cases, this atrophy-related syndrome occurs in response to lack of physical activity. It is expected that sedentary persons will begin losing lean mass as early as 25–30 years of age at a rate of 0.50%–0.75% annually. After age 50, the decline jumps to 15% with each decade, and after age 70, the decline further accelerates to a 30% loss in lean mass in subsequent decades. Lean mass atrophy can be reversed, slowed, or prevented with resistance training.

18. B. Amenorrhea, osteoporosis, and anorexia (the female triad) are symptoms that are often seen in female athletes with low body fat. This can lead to serious health consequences; these athletes should be referred to a qualified nutritionist and/or

psychologist for assistance and treatment. It is estimated that up to 60 percent of female athletes have disordered eating patterns but are not classified as having eating disorders. In many cases, those suffering from the female triad exercise excessively, often leading to injury and further weight-related problems.

CHAPTER 4

The National Federation of Professional Trainers

The National Federation of Professional Trainers (NFPT) was founded in 1988 and provides an impeccable certification credential that is among the most recognized in the industry. The NFPT is one of the most long-standing credentialing organizations in the industry. In the last 20 years, the NFPT has established more than 300 physical exam locations nationwide while purposely maintaining a comparatively small central office staff, making NFPT department heads more accessible.

What Are the NFPT's Objectives?

- To ensure that the graduate has an accredited, legally defensible, and trustworthy credential
- To provide an affordable, convenient, comprehensive, and applicable research-based education using state-of-the-art presentations

- To offer the most respected Certified Personal Trainer (CPT) credential for consumer/employer recognition of competence and professionalism
- To provide software, animated exercise demonstration, and ongoing continuing education information to Certified Personal Trainers for improved support services
- To facilitate and encourage the exchange of ideas, knowledge, business experiences, and financial opportunities among the NFPT's network of fitness trainer affiliates and professionals

Tell Me about the NFPT Certification Exam

Upon receipt of your application, the NFPT will send you the appropriate educational resource material to assist with exam preparation, along with a list of the closest test site locations. In approximately one week from your application, you will be provided with the following:

- *NFPT Study and Reference Manual*
- Choice of over 300 test site locations
- Software for client screening and consultation
- Nutrition and fitness prescription software
- All specialty course education manuals (available on CD-ROM)
- Technical support and access to a supplemental study guide
- State-of-the-art animated exercise demonstration

What Are the Prerequisites for NFPT Certification?

- Minimum age of 18
- High school diploma or equivalent
- Fitness-related experience (two or more years)

Talk to Me More about Exam Preparation

You will be given 60 days for independent home study and exam preparation; however, test date extensions can be granted in response to telephone or e-mail requests at no additional cost. A test due date extension can be given for up to one year past the original application date, and your examination appointment can be made any time prior to this test due date.

What's in the Study Guide?

The NFPT provides a study guide that is based on the NFPT's eight-week community college course. This guide allows you to independently prepare yourself to have a complete understanding of the *NFPT Study and Reference Manual* in an eight-week period of time. The guide is complete with worksheets, detailed chapter summaries, program design scenarios, assessment forms and guidelines, 320 practice questions, and more.

How Soon Do Candidates Receive Their Test Results?

If you choose a computer-based testing (CBT) exam location, you will receive a printout of your results instantly. Your certificate, membership card, and hard-copy score report will arrive by mail approximately two to three weeks after you successfully complete the examination.

What about Retesting?

The NFPT will provide a score report that indicates the highest- and lowest-ranking scores, which will be an indication of the categories that will need to be reviewed should a retest be necessary. The NFPT administrative retest fee is $60 in addition to the exam fee of either $20 (paper and pencil) or $44 (CBT).

What Enrollment and Payment Options Does the NFPT Offer?

The NFPT Certified Personal Trainer (CPT) course fee from start to finish will be no more than $499, regardless of the NFPT Enrollment Option. The core fee of $450 is supplemented by administrative exam charges that include a paper and pencil exam fee of $20 (collected at paper and pencil exam sites on exam day, if you choose to visit one), or a $44 CBT exam fee (paid by credit or debit card at the time that you schedule your test date). Test applicants also have the option of breaking up their course fee into two installments: $195 up front (to get access to the preparation material), with the balance of $255 due prior to taking the exam (within one year's time). One last option for those who are already employed by (or running) a health club is a full-price charge for the first applicant and a reduced rate of $295 for those who follow. Reduced-rate applicants will not receive hard copies of the study guide, but they can access the same material from the included CD-ROM or purchase it separately for $39.50.

What about Certification Renewal and Continuing Education?

The $85 per year membership renewal fee for an NFPT certified affiliate is among the lowest in the entire industry, and includes access to free-of-charge continuing education credits (CECs).

After your first full year of certification, you will be required to complete one CEC credit in each six-month period, or two credits per year. The NFPT posts self-tests every June and December that are available to NFPT certified affiliates through a membership ID number at www.nfpt.com.

Each self-test has a value of one credit, and each is made up of approximately 30 to 45 questions that are derived from articles posted monthly at NFPT's exclusive PersonalTrainerToday.com magazine and e-newsletter. These articles and self-tests are also made available in hard copy to those affiliates with little or no Internet access.

The process for completing NFPT self-tests requires the review of ongoing educational articles that assist in answering all self-test questions. The self-tests are extremely user-friendly and can be taken at any time within six months at your convenience. This method for obtaining CECs not only meets all regulated NCCA accreditation standards, but provides convenience and affordability that are difficult to find elsewhere.

How Is the NFPT Accredited?

The National Federation of Professional Trainers is one of the few elite organizations that have earned NCCA accreditation. The NFPT is the only NCCA-accredited certifying organization that provides continuing education credits as part of its certification renewal fee.

The NFPT Certified Personal Fitness Trainer Exam

How Is the Exam Broken Down?

The CPT exam was written using strict accreditation guidelines and statistical standards. This exam has 120 multiple-choice questions and is proctored in a monitored closed-book atmosphere with a time limit of two hours. The exam includes six assessed categories:

- Human anatomy
- Human physiology
- Exercise physiology
- Identifying the client's goals and implementing an appropriate exercise program
- Understanding characteristics of wellness
- Professional and legal practices

Fundamental Exam Emphasis Areas

The following are the emphasis areas (with percentage of focus) that you can expect to be asked about when preparing for and taking the NFPT certified personal trainer exam.

1. Apply the basic principles of human anatomy (15%)

   A. Understand the names and structure of the skeletal and muscular systems
   B. Name and define the following systems:
      1. Respiratory system
      2. Cardiovascular system
      3. Digestive system
   C. Identify types of joints
   D. Understand the principles of movement

2. Apply the basic principles of human physiology (20%)

    A. Understand the structure and function of the following systems and how they interact:
       1. Skeletal system
       2. Nervous system
       3. Muscular system
       4. Respiratory system
       5. Cardiovascular system
       6. Digestive system
       7. Endocrine system

    B. Identify the planes of motion

    C. Identify movements associated with joints:
       1. Agonistic
       2. Antagonistic

    D. Understand the types of muscle contractions:
       1. Concentric
       2. Eccentric
       3. Isometric

    E. Nutrition:
       1. Carbohydrates
       2. Fats
       3. Proteins
       4. Digestion and absorption of nutrients:
          a. Macronutrients
          b. Micronutrients

    F. Muscle fiber types:
       1. Red fast twitch

     2. Red slow twitch

     3. White fast twitch

  G. Energy systems:

     1. Aerobic

     2. Metabolic oxidation

     3. Anaerobic

  H. Factors affecting metabolic rate:

     1. Exogenous (external factors)

     2. Endogenous (internal factors)

3. Apply the basic principles of exercise physiology (25%)

  A. Apply training principles to the following activities:

     1. Resistance

     2. Cardiorespiratory

     3. Flexibility

     4. Recovery

  B. Understand training adaptations (the body's response to training):

     1. Anaerobic (e.g., strength, power, speed, endurance, and fatigue)

     2. Aerobic (e.g., speed, endurance, and fatigue)

  C. Apply fitness assessment techniques for the following fitness components:

     1. Body composition

     2. Aerobic

     3. Flexibility

     4. Anaerobic

     5. Recovery

D. Take heart rate and blood pressure measurements

E. Understand caloric intake and expenditure/energy balance

F. Recognize physical limitations [e.g., back, rotator cuff, knee, range of motion (ROM)]

G. Recognize or identify contraindicated exercises

H. Understand the energy continuum of exercise

I. Educate clients on proper hydration and fluid replacement techniques

4. Identify the client's goal and implement an exercise program (25%)

   A. Collect data using appropriate assessments

   B. Review data

   C. Synthesize data to assist with developing routines

   D. Define training methods:
      1. Anaerobic (e.g., repetition ranges, recovery, intensity)
      2. Aerobic [e.g., duration, frequency, speed, rating of perceived exertion (RPE)]

   E. Identify a realistic goal for the client

   F. Develop an exercise plan

   G. Determine special exercise conditions

   H. Implement the program

   I. Reevaluate the client, program, and goals

5. Understand the characteristics of wellness (10%)

   A. Absence of illness and disease

   B. Healthy lifestyle habits

C. Holistic health awareness (e.g., mind, body, and spirit)

D. Consequences of negative choices

E. Health benefits of exercise and physical activity

F. Weight management:

1. Exercise

2. Nutrition

G. Managing stress:

1. Physical

2. Emotional

3. Environmental

6. Professional and legal practices (5%)

A. Practice in an ethical manner

B. Participate in continuing education

C. Recognize professional limitations

D. Practice within legal limits

E. Collect appropriate documentation (e.g., hold harmless/liability waiver, physician waivers)

F. Maintain client confidentiality/privacy

G. Practice within professional scope/boundaries

H. Maintain cardiopulmonary resuscitation (CPR) certification

I. Maintain liability insurance

NFPT Sample Test Questions

(Answers can be found at the end of the sample test.)

1. Which system brings oxygen to body cells?

    A. Digestive
    B. Endocrine
    C. Cardiovascular
    D. Nervous

2. In what plane of motion is the arm moving during a military press?
    A. Frontal
    B. Sagittal
    C. Transverse
    D. Midsagittal

3. Which of the following is an example of a hinge joint?

    A. Shoulder
    B. Hip
    C. Spine
    D. Elbow

4. Which body system is responsible for the production of insulin?

    A. Endocrine
    B. Digestive
    C. Circulatory
    D. Lymphatic

5. Which of the following is the prime mover of the leg extension at the knee?

   A. Rectus femoris
   B. Pectoralis major
   C. Abductor brevis
   D. Rhomboid major

6. The heart is made up of which kind of muscle?

   A. Smooth
   B. Voluntary
   C. Cardiac
   D. Skeletal

7. Which type of circulation describes blood flow from the heart to the muscles and organs?

   A. Pulmonary
   B. Systemic
   C. Aerobic
   D. Anaerobic

8. The reason that a personal trainer needs to know a client's lean body weight through a body composition test is to

   A. determine what sport the client is best suited for.
   B. establish a caloric base to work from.

C. determine the client's strength level.

D. establish a base for cardio output.

9. The upright row should always be performed with caution and less intensity because:

A. it can cause a muscle imbalance between the biceps and the triceps.

B. it has been known to cause tears in the hamstrings and gastrocnemius.

C. simultaneous internal rotation and abduction of the shoulder can lead to impingement and tendon injury.

D. it's an advanced movement, and it can lead to overdevelopment of the pectoralis major and minor.

10. At 2% dehydration, the body's work capacity decreases by what percentage?

A. 12 to15

B. 20 to 30

C. 40 to 50

D. 60 to 70

11. Using the Karvonen formula, a 40-year-old man with a resting heart rate of 70 beats per minute who wants to train at 70% has a target of

A. 117 beats per minute.

B. 127 beats per minute.

C. 147 beats per minute.

D. 177 beats per minute.

12. A pregnant woman in the second trimester can safely perform all of the following exercises EXCEPT the

A. vertical chest press.

B. seated alternate dumbbell curls.

C. seated lateral raise.

D. flat bench press.

13. When collecting data, the trainer's primary tool overall is the

A. client questionnaire.

B. most recent exercise program.

C. body composition test.

D. urinary urine nitrogen (UUN).

14. When using the varied speed of motion, the slower the speed, the more emphasis is placed on pure

A. growth.

B. speed.

C. power.

D. stamina.

15. If the client has been inactive for at least one year, the personal trainer should

A. use past data to determine the client's new program.

B. reassess the client and determine new goals.

C. use her own personal judgment.

D. allow the client to determine his own program.

16. Compensatory acceleration refers to the development of

A. strength and stamina.

B. speed and power.

C. endurance and stamina.

D. strength and conditioning.

17. Which of the following may negatively affect a client's well-being?

A. Smoking

B. Balanced diet

C. Exercise

D. Adequate rest

18. For weight loss, a client should decrease her daily caloric intake by no more than how many calories a day?

A. 1,500

B. 1,000

C. 500

D. 100

19. The condition of good physical and mental health, when maintained by proper diet, exercise, and habits, is known as

   A. unhealthy living.
   B. aerobic conditioning.
   C. general health.
   D. athletic enhancement.

20. Lifestyle habits such as drug abuse, sedentary living, unsafe sex, poor diet, smoking, and violent behavior are all

   A. stress management techniques.
   B. elements of wellness.
   C. benefits of exercise.
   D. negative lifestyle choices.

21. Some of the possible health benefits of a good wellness program include

   A. an increase in overall health and a potentially longer lifespan.
   B. an increase in sickness and generally poor health.
   C. a lower energy level and an increase in overall stress.
   D. an inability to rest or sleep well.

22. Per 100 grams of commonly ingested proteins, what percentage is nitrogen?

A. 8%

B. 16%

C. 22%

D. 34%

23. A trainer should not train a client without which of the following documents being signed?

A. Confidentiality agreement

B. Facility rules and regulations

C. Informed consent waiver

D. CPR consent

24. Maintaining proper cardiopulmonary resuscitation (CPR) certification is beneficial for all of the following reasons EXCEPT

A. clients' safety.

B. professional liability.

C. insurance requirements.

D. client progress evaluation.

NFPT Sample Test Answers

1. C. Cardiovascular
2. A. Frontal
3. D. Elbow
4. A. Endocrine
5. A. Rectus femoris
6. C. Cardiac
7. B. Systemic
8. B. Establish a caloric base to work from
9. C. Simultaneous internal rotation and abduction of the shoulder can lead to impingement and tendon injury.
10. A. 12 to 15
11. C. 147 beats per minute
12. D. Flat bench press
13. A. Client questionnaire
14. A. Growth
15. B. Reassess the client and determine new goals
16. B. Speed and power
17. A. Smoking
18. C. 500
19. C. General health
20. D. Negative lifestyle choices
21. A. An increase in overall health and a potentially longer lifespan
22. B. 16%
23. C. Informed consent waiver
24. D. Client progress evaluation

5 | # The International Sports Sciences Association

I n 1988, a team of renowned fitness experts joined together under the leadership of Sal A. Arria, DC, MSS, and Frederick C. Hatfield, Ph.D., MSS, to stem the tide of physical decline.

Chosen from the elite ranks of research, coaching, sports medicine, and sports and fitness science, these individuals decided to draw a line in the sand and move toward a fitter and more healthy world.

The International Sports Sciences Association (ISSA) was formed with the mission of increasing the fitness of the people on our planet by helping more fitness professionals enjoy a successful career in fitness.

Tell Me about the International Sports Sciences Association and Its Philosophy

The International Sports Sciences Association believes that the health of our nation depends upon, and will be improved by, fitness professionals' ability to help people in their communities commit to a healthy lifestyle. The ISSA's efforts to stem the tide of poor health and physical decline are multiplied exponentially as ISSA graduates and members disseminate ISSA principles and methods to their clients, peers, and associates.

In its nationally accredited programs, ISSA teaches students and graduates how to construct scientifically proven, customized routines consisting of (1) cardiovascular conditioning, (2) resistance training, (3) flexibility and stability training, and (4) sound nutrition principles. In addition, ISSA trainers are taught that a well-constructed training program improves self-esteem and peace of mind, further enhancing the quality of life of each client.

Describe the ISSA Curriculum

ISSA's curriculum is a necessary mix of foundational principles and practical application. ISSA teaches the most current scientific information, beginning with anatomy, physiology, kinesiology, biomechanics, and exercise physiology. This solid foundation ensures that each student fully understands how the body moves and responds in order to best help the client.

Practical application—teaching the trainer to be a success in the real world—is ISSA's specialty. ISSA knows that in order to get the best training results, individualization is vital. Each student is taught how to assess a client's needs and then develop a custom program for that client.

The application of scientific knowledge to real-life challenges and goals is what clients are looking (and paying) for. Thus, ISSA teaches each student to develop the practical application of scientific principles for the purpose of meeting fitness goals.

A properly designed training program is key to helping clients reach their goals, but there is a mental component that plays a substantial role as well. ISSA trainers understand that the desire for transformation is rarely strictly physical.

Each client has his or her own individual life experiences and personal motivations that have caused him or her to seek the help of a fitness professional. ISSA emphasizes an approach to personal training that caters to both the emotional/mental and physical well-being of clients.

Though most of the ISSA certification programs and their curriculums are dedicated to the physical principles of training, ISSA provides students and trainers with a basic knowledge, comprehension, and appreciation of the impact that mental and emotional health can have on a client's overall success.

To encourage client accountability and program adherence, ISSA places great emphasis on a trainer's professional relationship with each client. The trainer must understand the importance of the client's personal journey—mental, emotional, and spiritual. This approach truly helps the client to establish the behavior modification necessary to effect lifelong change.

Throughout the learning process (which we know continues far into a trainer's career), ISSA is available to support its students and alumni. Learning is dynamic, and ISSA students and trainers can call ISSA professors at any time. Also, students and trainers can connect through the ISSA Member Forum and learn from one another what works and what doesn't. The ISSA believes in a community of learning.

The following is recently released updated material from the ISSA.

ISSA is the World Leader in Distance Education for Fitness

"New Study Shows Online Education Beats Classroom Study"

It's time you got some good news that you're not going to hear about in the media.

The U.S. Department of Education just released the findings of a meta-analysis conducted by its Office of Planning, Evaluation, and Policy Development that confirms what we at the ISSA have known for years:

"On average, students in online learning conditions performed better than those receiving face-to-face instruction."

This Department of Education report is important in that it's not the first study to support the benefits of online education, but, is significant in that an important branch of the federal government recognizes the power of online education.

Over the last several years, online education has gained tremendous momentum. A study by the Sloan Consortium found that nearly 4 million students were taking at least one course online. Since then, that number has increased each year by double digit percentages.

And there's a good reason.

Actually, LOTS of them.

Online Education Benefit #1: Flexibility that Fits Your Life

The Department of Education Report notes that the ability for students to use their time in a flexible manner boosted online education's popularity. Our ISSA students tell us that our online study flexibility is one of their favorite things why they chose the ISSA for their fitness certification.

Online Education Benefit #2: You Will Learn More, Quicker

Because you are studying when it's the best time for you, you simply will learn more, retain more and do so much quicker.

Online Education Benefit #3: You Save Time AND Money

By studying anytime you choose wherever you are, the cost savings in time, travel and money can be tremendous. Online education lets you say "Good-bye" to needing to go somewhere other than where you are to get your education.

Online Education Benefit #4: Access to World-Class Education Wherever You Are

Some of our students live in rural places or in areas that are geographically limited with access to higher education facilities. Yet they desire the world's best fitness education available. With online education, they get that education anywhere their computer is.

Online Education Benefit #5: Help and Be Helped by Others Just Like You

Imagine sharing fitness and nutrition ideas with your new friends in the UK or Japan. You can, anytime you want, with online education. Its 24/7/365 worldwide access makes the exchange of ideas as simple as an e-mail, message board or chat room conversation.

Online Education Benefit #6: Online Education Is Now and the Wave of the Future

The days of having to go to a "location" to get a world class education are over. Online education is the way the brightest and most successful students will learn anything they desire, whenever and wherever they desire that knowledge.

Online Education Benefit #7: Unlimited Opportunities to Learn and Grow

The ISSA will make a prediction: Once you get your ISSA Fitness Certification, you'll want to get your Specialty Certifications too. It happens to our students every day. They are so happy about how their ISSA Certification has changed their life and the lives of others that they don't want to stop learning. With online education and our great Specialty

Certification courses, their knowledge base can greatly multiply, at their own pace, and in the way that works best for their schedule and lives.

What Topics Are Included in the Program?

ISSA offers six fitness certification programs: Certified Fitness Trainer (CFT), Specialist in Performance Nutrition (SPN), Specialist in Sports Conditioning (SSC), Fitness Therapy (FT), Youth Fitness Trainer (YFT), and Specialist in Fitness for Older Adults (SFOA), in addition to dozens of carefully chosen continuing education courses. The ISSA flagship program—the Certified Fitness Trainer course—includes two texts and several learning tools, covering everything that is required to enjoy a career in the booming fitness industry.

The topics covered in the main text of the CFT course, *Fitness: The Complete Guide* (a 727-page resource), include anatomy, physiology, kinesiology, exercise-related biomechanics, client assessment, program development, strength training, nutrition, sample training and nutrition programs, exercise for special populations (older adults, those with chronic conditions, youth, and so on), an overview of sports medicine, and basic first aid. Program materials included with the CFT also cover the business side of personal training, teaching trainers how to succeed in the personal training industry.

Why Does the ISSA Believe This Is the Best Way to Teach Trainers How to Train Clients?

Being taught the practical application of academic principles not only helps ISSA students retain and apply the information that they learn, but also helps the population that ISSA trainers will serve. If ISSA trainers can impart information in a way that makes sense to their clients, it is more likely that those clients will understand the information and convert it into lasting change. Teaching clients to live and enjoy a healthy lifestyle, one that is designed specifically for each individual client, helps ensure long-term compliance, which, in turn, translates into long-lasting results.

Teaching ISSA students about the business aspects of personal training allows ISSA trainers to be financially successful while helping others. The right direction allows them to make a great living doing what they love. Also, successful trainers reach more people, furthering ISSA's goal of reversing physical decline in the United States and across the globe.

The ISSA offers multiple study options to allow students access to the ISSA program and, in turn, access to a personally and financially rewarding career. Online and at-home study and testing allow students to earn their certification from anywhere in the world, on their own schedules. Weekend seminars cater to students who benefit from interaction with a professor and offer the opportunity for proctored, closed-book examinations.

In addition to its fully accredited and award-winning curriculum, the ISSA also offers student support. Ongoing support allows students to continuously receive help and guidance on all topics, long after the successful completion of certification.

The ISSA's commitment to one-on-one support enhances student learning and enables ISSA trainers to help all of the clients they work with. It is this additional service that separates the ISSA from all other fitness organizations in the industry. It is another reason why more than 125,000 students in over 80 countries have chosen the ISSA.

Tell Me about the ISSA's Other Programs

Because the fitness and wellness industry is growing at an alarming rate, with large categories and subcategories sprouting new opportunities for personal trainers, ISSA has developed numerous specialized certifications: the Certified Fitness Trainer (CFT), Specialist in Fitness Nutrition (SPN), Specialist in Sports Conditioning (SSC), Fitness Therapy (FT), Youth Fitness Trainer (YFT), and Specialist in Fitness for Older Adults (SFOA). Specializations teach trainers how to work with older adults, youth, athletes, and clients with chronic conditions, as well as performance nutrition and many other areas. Specialized credentials translate into documented pay raises when the trainer is employed by a gym and an increased client base on which self-employed trainers can build their businesses.

The ISSA has also built an impressive continuing education library, covering topics such as gout, knee problems, creatine, caffeine, supplementation, and assorted business topics.

The ISSA ensures the success of its students by providing comprehensive scientific information about training, showing students how to apply that information in a practical way, teaching trainers how to succeed at the business aspects of personal training, providing a human contact from enrollment through certification, and offering an unmatched level of educational and professional support, free of charge.

What Kind of Support Does the ISSA Offer Its Members?

The ISSA's nationally accredited curriculum with full tuition protection covers a range of useful topics that will serve the fitness professional for a lifetime. This dedication to cutting-edge resources is supported by a rock-solid corporate team, including the Student Services Department, the Educational Support Department, and the Professional Support staff.

Student Services, Educational Support, and Professional Support have one mission: to serve the ISSA student and trainer. Student Services is available to answer any questions about continuing education, corequisites, seminar attendance, and student records. The Educational and Professional Support teams are available to help students succeed both academically and professionally.

To gauge how best to serve its students, the ISSA continually evaluates its programs, services, and alumni success with the help of its members and their employers. The ISSA not only welcomes student feedback and suggestions, but actively seeks student input through evaluations and surveys. The ISSA also collaborates with gym owners nationwide to be sure it is teaching students how best to succeed in the real world.

All active students have free access to Educational Support via a toll-free phone number, e-mail, and an online question board. Educational Support is available to answer any questions about the course material, to offer studying advice, or simply to motivate students.

The ISSA offers many services to all active certified trainers. Starting with free access to the job board (www.ISSAtrainer.com) containing hundreds of nationwide job opportunities, the ISSA takes an active role in helping students find employment after certification.

To help ISSA trainers with clients, Professional Support is available via a toll-free phone number, by e-mail, or through an active online question board. Unlimited use of Professional Support is available to help with all aspects of a training career, programming for unique clients, the business aspects of personal training, and even advice on how trainers can reach their personal fitness goals.

What Distinguishes the ISSA from Other Certification Organizations?

Two things set the ISSA apart in the fitness industry: federally recognized accreditation and service.

The ISSA is fully accredited by the Accrediting Commission of the Distance Education and Training Council (DETC), a nationally recognized accrediting agency that is a recognized member of the Council for Higher Education Accreditation (CHEA). The ISSA is the first fitness organization to earn national accreditation from a federally recognized accrediting agency.

The secretary of education is required by law to publish a list of nationally recognized accrediting agencies, and the Accrediting Commission of the DETC is on that list. These agencies have been determined by the secretary to reliably evaluate the quality of education provided by institutions of higher education.

The Accrediting Commission of the DETC is also a recognized member of the Council for Higher Education Accreditation. The CHEA is a private nonprofit national organization that coordinates accreditation activity in the United States. Recognition by the CHEA affirms that the standards and processes of accrediting organizations are consistent with the quality, improvement, and accountability expectations of the CHEA.

The ISSA is now approved by the U.S. Department of Defense for Military Tuition Assistance through the DANTES, AVOTEC, and MyCAA (the Military Spouse Career Advancement Account) programs.

These programs provide military personnel with the opportunity to gain their education and certification (even multiple ISSA specialized training courses) from the ISSA so that they can enter the workforce and start an exciting career as a fitness professional with the best credentials in the industry.

The ISSA believes that a U.S. DoE- and CHEA-recognized accreditation helps to legitimize the public perception of fitness educators, and gives the entire profession more credibility as wellness providers. The ISSA also believes that DETC accreditation is congruent with the International Health, Racquet and Sportsclub Association's (IHRSA's) mission to "protect and promote the health and fitness industry."

Why Not NCCA Accreditation?

The NCCA is not recognized by either the U.S. DoE or CHEA. Further, NCCA standards specifically state that any organization that seeks accreditation for its examination cannot require candidates to take any of its courses, classes, training, or workshops as a prerequisite to sitting for the examination. The NCCA also does not accredit institutions of higher learning or educational programs, only exams.

The ISSA believes that students should be required to complete specific educational courses, classes, and training prior to taking an examination to become a personal trainer. It is for these reasons that ISSA has chosen not to pursue NCCA accreditation.

What Are the ISSA's Continuing Education Requirements?

The ISSA requires 20 CEUs of continuing education every two years to maintain certification. As with any allied or medical profession, the ISSA also believes that the public is best served when certified personal trainers keep up on the latest information and stay current with new research in their profession.

What Are the Study and Testing Options?

Students receive hard-copy materials and full online access to materials and support. They can complete their course work entirely by mail or entirely online. Also, students can supplement their learning with a weekend seminar and take a closed-book, proctored exam.

Even though the program is self-paced, enrolled students are not alone. ISSA's Member Forum provides a place where students and trainers can ask questions and receive input from ISSA Educational and Professional Support as well as from fellow fitness professionals. Also, active students and trainers have unlimited access to one-on-one educational and professional support via toll-free phone line or e-mail.

ISSA Sample Test

Multiple-Choice Questions

(Answers can be found at the end of the chapter.)

1. Which of the following would be considered anaerobic metabolism?

   A. ATP/CP pathway
   B. Nonoxidative glycolytic pathway
   C. Oxidative pathway
   D. A and B
   E. B and C
   F. A and C

2. High-repetition resistance training

    A. does not innervate high-threshold motor units.
    B. innervates high-threshold motor units.
    C. limits the potential for Type IIB muscle fiber hypertrophy.
    D. A and C.
    E. B and C.

3. This principle states that our bodies will physiologically adapt according to whether we are training aerobically or anaerobically.

    A. The SAID principle
    B. The principle of individual differences
    C. The FITT principle
    D. The specificity principle
    E. The GAS principle

4. An example of a prime mover is

    A. the biceps muscle during a biceps curl.
    B. internal and external oblique muscles during a crunch.
    C. the triceps during a biceps curl.
    D. the pronator teres during pronation.
    E. none of the above.

5. How many calories equal one gram of carbohydrates?

A. 0

B. 1

C. 2

D. 4

E. 9

6. What is the primary muscle used in a hammer curl?

A. Pectoralis major

B. Biceps muscle

C. Latissimus dorsi

D. Gastrocnemius

E. Trapezius

7. Name an alternative exercise for the hammer curl.

A. Squat

B. Preacher curl

C. Calf raise

D. Push-ups

E. Crunches

8. Name the origin of the primary muscle used in a hammer curl.

A. Groove of the humerus

B. Olecranon process of the ulna

C. Patella

D. Medial surface of the tibia

E. None of the above

Case Study

The ISSA places a strong emphasis on case study, which calls on the student to design a program for a sample client. Included is a case study and sample answer from its practice exam. The case study helps the ISSA evaluate trainer competence, so while the ISSA wouldn't want to publish a sample answer to the case studies that are in the official exam, the following case study is very similar to those in the official exam.

Case Study: Jocko Johnson

Client Profile:

Client profile: Jocko Johnson

Age: 30

Gender: Male

Resting heart rate: 70 bpm

Height: 6′1″

Weight: 200 lb

Body fat percentage: 18%

Jocko was an athlete in high school, playing a variety of sports, including football, track (100- and 400-meter events), and baseball. He has come to you because he has recently had his 30th birthday and wants to get back in shape. While he is in decent shape already, Jocko wishes to get in excellent shape with an eye on perhaps competing in a local bodybuilding show in the future.

Client Calculations

1. Using the information given, calculate the client's BMI: **26.4**

2. Calculate the client's BMR: **2,073**

3. Calculate the client's target heart rate at 60% and 80% using the Karvonen formula: **154** *(Author Note: The Karvonen formula is described differently by each organization in its materials. It's essentially a mathematical formula that involves using your maximum heart rate minus your age in order to find a target heart range [which is a percentage of your maximum heart rate] at which to exercise.)*

Assessment, Training, and Nutritional Strategy

Using the information given, address points a–c.

a. Discuss fitness tests or methods of evaluation that should be used to assess the client, providing the rationale for your recommendations. Be sure to address the specific conditions presented by your client.

While Jocko may appear to be a dream client on the surface, I realize that his athletic background and recent birthday could lead to more than a little impatience on his part. At my initial consultation, I would explain to him that I would need at least a three-month commitment from him to ensure his getting started on the right foot. Most clients need this amount of time to really get into the swing of things and start seeing some results. I would establish my fees at our initial meeting, get him signed up, give him a health history questionnaire to fill out for our next meeting, and set up our first appointment.

For our first appointment, I would plan on having enough time to have Jocko complete a release of liability form and to go over his health history questionnaire. If he had any red flags or other concerns, we would hold off on training until I had spoken to his doctor and his doctor had released him for exercise. If his health history looked good, we would get started on the enclosed program.

To track Jocko's progress, I would perform circumference, body weight, and body fat percentage measurements. Also, we would gauge Jocko's starting level of fitness with an upper and lower body 1RM test, a 12-minute run-walk test, a zipper stretch test, and a sit-and-reach test.

b. Provide a detailed, comprehensive, 12-week periodized training program, including specific sets, repetitions, and exercises, utilizing an integrated approach.

Weeks 1–3
The following exercises are to be performed in a circuit fashion on Monday, Wednesday, and Friday.

Exercise	Reps	Sets
Squat/leg press	10–15	1–2
Incline bench press	10–15	1–2

Leg curl	10–15	1–2
T-bar row	10–15	1–2
Standing calf raises	10–15	1–2
DB shoulder press	10–15	1–2
Crunches	20	1–2
Seated DB curl	10–15	1–2
Back extensions	15	1–2
Cable pushdowns	10–15	1–2

Tuesday/Thursday: 20- to 45-minute run

Saturday: 30-second jog/30-second sprint for 5 minutes total

Figure 5.1 **Weeks 4–9**

Mesocycle Split

Monday	*Wednesday*	*Friday*
Quads	Pecs	Biceps
Hamstrings	Back	Triceps
Calves	Abs/lower back	Shoulders

Exercises, Reps, and Sets

Monday			*Wednesday*			*Friday*		
Exercise	**Reps**	**Sets**	**Exercise**	**Reps**	**Sets**	**Exercise**	**Reps**	**Sets**
Squat	8–10	4	Incline bench			Pull-up	8–10	4
Stiff leg deadlift	8–10	4	press (a1)	8–10	4	Cable rows	8–10	3
Leg extension	12	2	Peck deck	12	2	Lying tri		
Leg curls (a2)	12	2	Preacher curls	10–12	2	extensions	8–10	3
Seated calf raises	10	2	Russian twist	8	3	DB shoulder press	8–10	2
Standing calf raises	12	2	Back extensions	10	3	Lateral raises	8–10	2

Note: a1 and a2 designate two exercises that are to be done in a superset fashion. Do one set of the a1 exercise and while you are resting, perform one set of the a2 exercise. Repeat until you have completed all prescribed sets for those exercises before moving on to the next exercise(s).

Tuesday: 30-second jog/30-second sprint, start 5 minutes and add 1 minute each week

Thursday: 30- to 45-minute run

Saturday: 30-second jog/30-second sprint, start 5 minutes and add 1 minute each week

Figure 5.2 **Weeks 10–12**

Mesocycle split

Monday	Wednesday	Friday
Quads	Pecs	Biceps
Hamstrings	Back	Triceps
Calves	Abs/Lower Back	Shoulders

Exercises, Reps, and Sets

Monday			Wednesday			Friday		
Exercise	Reps	Sets	Exercise	Reps	Sets	Exercise	Reps	Sets
Deadlift	8	6	Bench press (a1)	8	6	Barbell curl (a1)	10	5
Stiff leg deadlift	8	4	Pull-up (a2)	8	6	Close grip bench (a2)	10	5
Seated calf raises	8	5	Russian twist	8	3	Military press	10	5
			Back extensions	8	3			

Note: a1 and a2 designate two exercises that are to be done in a superset fashion. Do one set of the a1 exercise and while you are resting, perform one set of the a2 exercise. Repeat until you have completed all prescribed sets for those exercises before moving on to the next exercise(s).

Tuesday: 30-second jog/30-second sprint, start 5 minutes and add 1 minute each week

Thursday: 30-minute run

Saturday: 30-second jog/30-second sprint, start 10 minutes and add 1 minute each week

c. Discuss nutritional strategies, and supplement recommendations with a rationale for your choices.

My nutritional strategy for this client would consist of five high-calorie days and two low-calorie days. I would suggest that he follow a 1-2-3 or 1-2-4 macronutrient ratio, depending on his metabolism and mesocycle. The higher-intensity mesocycles would warrant more carbs, while the lower-intensity ones would not need as much fuel. I would suggest that he get around 160 grams of protein a day and get his fat from "healthy" fats, such as olive oil and hemp seed oil. The easiest way to estimate his daily caloric requirements is to have him keep a food log for a few days and see where he is at now. It will be much easier to make adjustments to his diet with a reference point.

Multiple-Choice Answers

1. D. A and B
2. D. A and C
3. A. The SAID principle
4. A. The biceps muscle during a biceps curl
5. D. 4
6. B. Biceps muscle
7. B. Preacher curl
8. E. None of the above

CHAPTER 6

National Strength and Conditioning Association

The National Strength and Conditioning Association-Certified Personal Trainer (NSCA-CPT) certification was developed in 1993 for professionals who work one-on-one with their clients in a variety of environments, including health/fitness clubs, wellness centers, schools, and clients' homes. The exam thoroughly tests the knowledge and skills that are necessary to successfully train both active and sedentary physically healthy individuals, and also individuals with special needs, such as the elderly and obese. Personal trainers with specialized expertise may also be involved in training clients with orthopedic, cardiovascular, and other chronic conditions.

Today, more than 10,000 fitness professionals around the world hold this prestigious credential. The NSCA-CPT became the first personal training credential to be nationally accredited by the National Commission for Certifying Agencies (NCCA) in 1996, and it has continued to set the standard for personal training as the best-respected personal trainer certification through national and international recognition. The NSCA has 34,000 members in 70 countries.

Tell Me about the NSCA Certification Programs

The NSCA-CPT credential is designed for professionals who work one-on-one with their clients in a variety of environments, including YMCAs, schools, health/fitness clubs, and clients' homes. NSCA-CPT examination candidates must be CPR certified to sit for the exam.

Certified Strength and Conditioning Specialist Program

In addition to the CPT certification, the NSCA also offers a Certified Strength and Conditioning Specialist (CSCS) program. Both certifications are highly recognized and respected in today's competitive marketplace and have been accredited by the NCCA since 1996.

The CSCS program was initiated in 1985 to identify individuals who have the knowledge and skills to design and implement safe and effective strength and conditioning programs. The program encourages a higher level of competence among practitioners, which, in turn, raises the quality of the strength training and conditioning programs provided by those who are CSCS certified. To be eligible to take the exam, you must hold a BA/BS degree, be enrolled as a college senior at an accredited college or university, or hold a degree in chiropractic medicine, and be CPR certified.

What Are the NSCA Certified Personal Trainer Exam Prerequisites?

Although no formal postsecondary course work is required, candidates are expected to have a good knowledge of biomechanical concepts, training adaptations, anatomy, exercise physiology, program design guidelines, and current position papers pertaining to special populations.

To qualify to register for the NSCA-CPT exam, you must be at least 18 years old and have a high school diploma or equivalent.

Current CPR and AED certification is also a requirement. However, if you do not have current CPR and AED certification, you can still register for and take the NSCA-CPT exam. The NSCA certification will accept any adult CPR and AED certification obtained by attending a CPR and AED course that meets the following criteria:

- Must have a hands-on training component (certification through a course completed entirely online will not be accepted).
- Must include a skills performance evaluation.
- Examples of accepted CPR and AED certifications include
  - American Heart Association (Heartsaver)
  - Red Cross (including Blended Learning First Aid/CPR/ AED Program)
  - National Safety Council
  - St. John Ambulance

How Do I Register for the Exam?

Exams are offered in two formats: a paper and pencil version that is administered worldwide, and a computer-based version that is offered only in the United States. The registration for the exam is simple and allows the NSCA to keep the candidate informed.

Paper and Pencil Format

1. Determine which exam you wish to register for, and be sure you meet the prerequisites.

2. Complete the exam registration form online or in paper and pencil form.

3. Submit your registration by the early deadline for the lowest exam fee; registrations will not be accepted after the registration cutoff date.

4. If you register online, you will be sent a confirmation e-mail. To register by mail, complete the registration form found in the Downloads section of the online Resources section.

5. One month before the exam date, you will be sent your official confirmation notice in the mail, indicating the site and date you are registered for and a link to the Candidate Handbook.

6. Download and read the appropriate *Exam Candidate Handbook* from the online Resources section.

7. One week before the exam date, you will receive a test center admission letter for each section of the exam for which you are registered (the CSCS exam has two sections; the NSCA-CPT exam has one section), indicating the institution, building name, and room number. Review the admission letter(s) carefully and contact the Exam Registration Department at ext. 103 or 118 if it contains errors.

Computer-Based Format

1. Determine which exam you wish to register for, and be sure you meet the prerequisites.

2. Download and read the appropriate *Exam Candidate Handbook* from the online Resources section.

3. Complete the online exam registration form. (Computer-based exam registrations can be completed only online.)

4. You will be sent two confirmation e-mails. The first will be sent instantly, upon receipt of your registration. The second will be sent within five business days and will contain information on scheduling an appointment with the testing service.

Special Accommodations

A candidate may request special accommodations if she has a medical condition that will prevent her from taking the exam as it is typically administered. The candidate initiates this request, and prior to the exam, the testing agency will contact the candidate with information about the accommodations that will be provided.

Exams on Request

NSCA Certification will make all the arrangements necessary for the exam and will assist in promoting the exam. However, it is the responsibility of the host to ensure that at least 10 candidates register for the exam. The Exam Registration Department will provide a Letter of Guarantee that explains the responsibilities of the exam host and NSCA Certification for an Exam on Request (EOR).

Hosting an exam will provide advantages for the NSCA, the host, and the individual candidates. Hosts will earn CEUs and receive access to grouped data summaries of candidates' performance, while candidates are able to take the exam at a convenient location.

What Are the Costs?

Member costs:

Student	$95.00 with verification
Professional	$120.00
Certified	$115.00

What Benefits Do NSCA Members Receive?

Beyond the distinction of having an NSCA certification, members also receive NSCA publications, research, and journals. Additionally, NSCA members will have access to the following:

- *Career and Leadership Development Center.* This Web site was developed to bring to NSCA members the experience accumulated by authorities in leadership and recognized strength and conditioning professionals. Articles were contributed for the purpose of providing members with insights and guidance. The job board allows members to search for employment and employers to find the most qualified individuals.
- *Conferences, symposia, and clinics.* NSCA conferences are an exceptional way to learn the latest research, techniques, and breakthrough performance methods used by top professionals throughout the world. They are gatherings of strength, conditioning, research, and sports medicine professionals, featuring dynamic speakers, unique presentations, and interactive oppor-

tunities with established strength and conditioning professionals from around the world. All NSCA conferences provide CSCS and NSCA-CPT continuing education unit (CEU) opportunities.

- *NSCA involvement.* The NSCA offers career enhancement opportunities that include volunteering for one of the NSCA committees, representing your state as a state/provincial director, serving on the board of directors, publishing an article in the *Journal of Strength and Conditioning Research* or the *Strength and Conditioning Journal*, participating in a special interest group, and presenting at or attending an NSCA conference and clinic.
- *Grants and scholarships.* The National Strength and Conditioning Association financially supports the higher education of students pursuing a career in the strength and conditioning field, and facilitates and disseminates strength and conditioning research. This is done by awarding grants and scholarships. The grants that are awarded are the GNC Nutritional Research grant, graduate research—master's and doctoral grants, and the Young Investigator grant. The scholarships that are awarded are the high school, Minority Power Systems Professional, Challenge, and Women's scholarships.

  All grant and scholarship applicants must be NSCA members for at least one year prior to the application deadline, and must be pursuing careers in strength and conditioning. Members are not eligible to win more than one scholarship or grant in any given year.
- *NSCA catalog.* The NSCA Online Store supports the mission of the NSCA and provides products to help NSCA members promote and enhance their careers.

- *Certified Professional with Insurance (CPI) Membership*. Coverage is limited to members acting in the capacity of a Certified Strength and Conditioning Specialist (CSCS) or NSCA-Certified Personal Trainer (NSCA-CPT). Only U.S., U.S. territories (Puerto Rico, Virgin Islands), and Canadian residents may purchase insurance. Institutions may not purchase insurance. There is no group liability insurance available. This policy will not cover a place of business, employee, or coworker. It protects against suits for activities anywhere in the world, provided the original suit is brought within the United States, its territories or possessions, or Canada.

- *Additional Insured*. An Additional Insured, such as a gym, school, or other facility, provides insurance coverage for that gym, school, or other facility for *your* activities. If the gym, school, or other facility is named as a defendant in an action involving your training activities, the insurance will provide defense and/or indemnification. The Additional Insured program is not for a personal business premises. Only current CPI members who are U.S., U.S. territories, or Canadian residents may purchase this insurance.

    An Additional Insured can be added to your policy at any time during the insurance period for a cost of $50 per facility. Each individual facility must be named as an Additional Insured, as one insured will not cover other facilities. Additional Insured costs are not prorated, and the dates run from February 1 to January 31 each year in conjunction with the CPI membership.

NSCA Professional Recognition

- *Registered Strength and Conditioning Coach*. The NSCA has created a registry of qualified members who are interested in better defining a career path in strength and conditioning. The purpose of the registry is to recognize coaches who have been certified as strength and conditioning specialists (CSCS), have demonstrated commitment to the field of strength and conditioning, and wish to be identified for career advancement.

- *Coach Practitioner distinction.* NSCA members who have received the CSCS certification can apply for the Coach Practitioner distinction. The purpose of this distinction is to encourage high standards of professional practice and responsibility in the field of strength and conditioning, and to distinguish this profession as an applied specialty area. The Coach Practitioner distinction is designed to identify and reward experienced strength and conditioning professionals who train athletes at the professional, collegiate, and high school levels. Coach Practitioners are recognized by the NSCA as elite-level strength and conditioning professionals and receive the NSCA's highest level of distinction, NSCA Professional Recognition.

- *NSCA Personal Trainer—Advanced Recognition.* NSCA members who are Certified Personal Trainers may earn this recognition through their contribution to the fitness industry and the NSCA.

- *NSCA Fellow.* The NSCA Fellow (FNSCA) designation is awarded to those strength and conditioning professionals who have demonstrated a sustained contribution to the NSCA and supported its mission.

The NSCA-CPT Exam

To earn the NSCA-CPT credential, candidates are required to pass a three-hour exam. The first 35 questions are based on a video that assesses knowledge primarily in the areas of exercise techniques, functional anatomy, and fitness testing protocols.

This exam contains 28 questions on client consultation/fitness assessment, 49 questions on program planning, 49 questions on exercise techniques, and 14 questions on safety/emergency issues.

To ensure that the NSCA-CPT exam reflects current job-related duties, new questions are continuously introduced and "pretested." Pretesting is accomplished by interspersing 10 new ("untried") questions throughout the exam. Only this small number is included so that exam candidates will not need additional testing time. These questions are not scored as part of a candidate's certification exam, and they do not affect an individual's pass/fail status. The nonscored questions are scattered throughout the exam so that candidates will answer them with the same effort that they give to the actual scored questions.

NSCA Exam Breakdown

The NSCA-CPT exams are broken down into four areas:

1. Client consultation and assessment

2. Program planning

3. Techniques of exercise

4. Safety, emergency procedures, and legal issues

The following are exam questions taken from the NSCA-CPT Practice Exam Guides (1-2-3), which can be purchased at the www.nsca-lift.org Web site. (Answers can be found at the end of the chapter.)

NSCA Practice Questions

Client Consultation and Assessment

1. When should the personal trainer administer an informed consent form to a client?

   A. Before the fitness evaluation
   B. After the first exercise session
   C. During the physician's medical examination
   D. Immediately after reviewing the fitness evaluation results

2. A male client completed a medical history form. Which of the following responses should prompt the personal trainer to require the client to have a diagnostic medical exam prior to beginning a vigorous (>60% VO_2 max) aerobic exercise program?

   I. One resting blood pressure reading of 128/88.
   II. The client is currently 29 years old.
   III. The client's father experienced a heart attack at age 52.
   IV. A recently tested serum HDL level of 30 mg/dL.

   A. I and III only
   B. II and IV only
   C. I and II only
   D. III and IV only

3. A 5'6" (168-cm), 188-pound (85-kg), 44-year-old man wants to begin exercising. His personal trainer discovers that the client has no history of disease, but he has never participated in

a formal exercise program. A fitness evaluation revealed the following results:

I. Partial curl-up test: 65
II. Body mass index: 30.1
III. 1.5-mile run time (minutes:seconds): 12:45
IV. Estimated 1RM bench press: 115 pounds (52 kg)

Which of these results indicate a deficient or undesirable score that the personal trainer should give attention to when developing this client's initial exercise program?

    A. I and III only
    B. II and IV only
    C. I and II only
    D. III and IV only

4. The female athlete triad consists of all of the following conditions or behaviors EXCEPT

    A. disordered eating.
    B. amenorrhea.
    C. osteoporosis.
    D. hypoglycemia.

5. Which of the following is an example of a fitness evaluation test result that describes a client's relative muscular strength?

A. Shoulder press (maximum load for one repetition)

B. Push-ups (maximum number of consecutive repetitions)

C. Bench press (maximum load divided by the client's body weight)

D. Back squat (maximum load for five repetitions multiplied by the client's body weight)

6. A female client complains of increased fatigue and irritability in the late morning of each workday. A dietary analysis reveals that the client's breakfast typically consists of a jelly donut and a regular soft drink. Which of the following suggestions should the personal trainer recommend to alleviate the client's lethargic and irritable demeanor?

A. Drink a cup of coffee mid-morning

B. Substitute a diet soft drink for the regular soft drink

C. Replace foods to increase complex carbohydrate intake

D. Eat breakfast earlier in the morning

7. Which of the following describes when the personal trainer administers the client–personal trainer–fitness facility agreement to the client?

A. Before the client purchases sessions

B. During the health appraisal screening

C. At the initial client consultation meeting

D. After the goal-setting process

8. Which of the following behaviors characterizes anorexia, but NOT bulimia?

   A. Preoccupation with food
   B. Recurrent episodes of binge eating
   C. Irregular eating pattern
   D. Continual refusal to gain body weight

9. Which of the following should be a part of the initial interview with a new client?

   A. Performing the PAR-Q evaluation
   B. Performing fitness testing
   C. Completing the client–trainer agreement
   D. Completing the medical history form

10. Which of the following describes when the personal trainer should administer the medical history form to the client?

   A. Before the client purchases sessions
   B. During the health appraisal screening
   C. At the initial client consultation meeting
   D. After the goal-setting process

Program Planning

11. During the initial interview, a client states that she enjoys riding her bike for exercise. The personal trainer and client agree that biking will be included in the exercise program as long as

the client attends all her scheduled workouts each week. After the client misses one of her scheduled sessions, the personal trainer removes biking and replaces it with running. Which of the following techniques was used to motivate the client to attend her exercise sessions?

A. Positive reinforcement
B. Negative reinforcement
C. Positive punishment
D. Negative punishment

12. Which of the following is a chronic training adaptation to a six-month aerobic exercise program composed of three 30-minute sessions per week at 70–85% of a client's maximum heart rate?

A. Decreased left ventricular volume
B. Increased total blood hemoglobin levels
C. Decreased capillary density in trained muscles
D. Increased breathing frequency during submaximal exercise

13. Which of the following is an appropriate INITIAL load and repetition scheme for an untrained client who has an estimated 1RM of 250 pounds (114 kg) for the leg press exercise?

Load	Repetitions
A. 160 pounds (73 kg)	5
B. 160 pounds (73 kg)	15
C. 210 pounds (95 kg)	5
D. 210 pounds (95 kg)	15

14. A client with a patellofemoral knee injury is referred to a personal trainer by a physical therapist. The physical therapist recommends that the client perform exercises that do NOT permit more than 60 degrees of knee flexion. Which of the following exercises would be the MOST appropriate for the personal trainer to include in the client's program?

    A. Quarter squat
    B. Leg extension
    C. Deadlift with dumbbells
    D. Forward step lunge

15. A moderate-intensity (8 to 12 RM loads) resistance training program involving one-minute rest periods between sets and exercises is designed PRIMARILY to improve a client's

    A. strength.
    B. hypertrophy.
    C. explosive power.
    D. aerobic endurance.

16. A client has been participating in a resistance training program for the past 3 months. During her last three sessions, she completed the following workout:

	Session 1	Session 2	Session 3
Exercise	(load × reps)	(load × reps)	(load × reps)
Bench press	65 × 10	65 × 12	65 × 12
Lat pulldown	45 × 9	45 × 11	45 × 10
Shoulder press	20 × 11	20 × 12	20 × 11

If her repetition goal is 10 for each set, what loads should this client use for the next session?

	Bench press	Lat pulldown	Shoulder press
A.	75	50	25
B.	70	45	20
C.	65	45	25
D.	70	40	30

17. Which of the following exercises would be the MOST effective for increasing the vertebral bone mineral density of a client who is at risk for osteoporosis?

A. Leg extension
B. Bent over row
C. Back extension
D. Front squat

Scenario 1 (questions 18–20)

After following a regular jogging program for a year, a 40-year-old man decides to hire a personal trainer to help him prepare for his first 10-km (6.2-mile) road race. Although this client has Type 1 diabetes, he had a recent physical examination and has been cleared by his physician to continue exercising. His initial fitness evaluation revealed these results:

Height:	5′10″ (178 cm)
Weight:	175 pounds (80 kg)
Resting heart rate:	80 bpm
Body fat:	15%

12-minute run:	1.6 miles (2.6 km)
Push-ups (maximum):	25
Sit-and-reach test:	+1 inch (+2.5 cm)

18. Based upon his fitness evaluation results, the personal trainer should encourage this client to improve his

   A. cardiovascular endurance.
   B. back and hip flexibility.
   C. body composition.
   D. upper body muscular fitness.

19. Which of the following systems will be affected the MOST during the INITIAL stage of aerobic training for this client?

   A. Neuromuscular
   B. Cardiorespiratory
   C. Endocrine
   D. Psychological

20. Which of the following pre-exercise strategies would be the MOST effective in preventing this client from becoming hypoglycemic during the 10-km race?

   A. Increase insulin dosage
   B. Increase carbohydrate intake
   C. Inject insulin into the gluteals
   D. Drink at least 12 ounces (355 mL) of water

Techniques of Exercise

21. Which of the following stair-climbing techniques results in the greatest DECREASE in relative exercise intensity?

    A. Positioning only the balls of the feet on the pedals
    B. Supporting the upper body with hands on the rails
    C. Swinging the arms at the sides in a running motion
    D. Allowing the pedals to consistently rise to their highest position

22. A personal trainer instructs a client to perform a diagonal lunge. Which of the following muscles or muscle groups provides the LEAST eccentric assistance for the lead leg during the forward movement phase?

    A. Hamstrings
    B. Quadriceps
    C. Gluteus maximus
    D. Gluteus medius

23. Which of the following drills would be the MOST appropriate for a personal trainer to include in a beginning plyometric program?

    A. One-leg lateral hop
    B. Squat jump
    C. Alternate leg bound
    D. Depth jump

24. A personal trainer would like to include stability ball exercises in an exercise program. Which of the following guidelines should the personal trainer use to determine the proper stability ball size?

    A. When sitting on the ball, the client's hips and knees should be flexed to 90 degrees.

    B. When sitting on the ball, only the client's toes should touch the floor.

    C. When standing next to the ball, the top of the ball should be lower than the client's knees.

    D. When standing next to the ball, the top of the ball should be level with the client's anterior superior iliac spine (ASIS).

25. When teaching a client to perform a depth jump, the personal trainer should instruct the client to focus on which of the following?

    A. Minimizing amortization phase time

    B. Maximizing eccentric phase time

    C. Maximizing horizontal movement

    D. Minimizing vertical movement

26. Which of the following is an appropriate technique guideline to give to a client who is beginning a jogging program?

    A. Minimize side-to-side arm swing.

    B. Focus the eyes on the ground just in front of the feet.

    C. Bring the feet up and back to touch the heels to the buttocks.

    D. Contact the ground with the balls of the feet first.

27. Which of the following modes of exercise should a personal trainer recommend to a client who wants to involve as many muscle groups as possible during a single cardiovascular workout?

    A. Rowing machine
    B. Distance running
    C. Mountain biking
    D. Race walking

28. A personal trainer offers free sessions to clients who achieve their goals within a predetermined amount of time. Which of the following describes this motivational technique?

    A. Intrinsic motivation
    B. Achievement motivation
    C. Positive reinforcement
    D. Positive punishment

29. Which of the following describes the primary and secondary factors that dictate the predominant energy system used during an exercise session?

	Primary	Secondary
A.	Exercise mode	Energy stores
B.	Exercise duration	Exercise intensity
C.	Exercise intensity	Exercise duration
D.	Energy stores	Exercise mode

30. Which of the following is an open kinetic chain exercise?

A. Push-up

B. Leg curl

C. Stationary lunge

D. Seated calf raise

Safety, Emergency Procedures, and Legal Issues

31. During a personal training session in a client's home, the client's 15-year-old daughter enters the exercise room, trips on the base of the client's weight bench, falls, and is injured. Which of the following parties may be legally responsible?

    I. The client's daughter

    II. The personal trainer

    III. The client

    IV. The manufacturer of the weight bench

    A. II only

    B. II and III only

    C. I and IV only

    D. I, III, and IV only

32. All of the following are possible indicators of a client's becoming overtrained EXCEPT:

    A. increased exercise capacity during submaximal exercise.

    B. decreased body fat percentage.

    C. increased diastolic blood pressure at rest.

    D. decreased motor coordination and agility.

Scenario 2 (question 33)

A 33-year-old, 5'1" (155-cm) woman has been working with a personal trainer for six months. During that time, the client's primary modes of exercise have been walking and jogging in an effort to lower her percentage of body fat. Her *initial* and *most recent* body composition tests revealed these results:

	January 1	June 30
Body weight:	130 pounds (59 kg)	124 pounds (56 kg)
Body fat:	30%	25%

33. The client states that she wants to add resistance training to her program. During the first resistance training session, she sprains her ankle on her lead foot while stepping out on the forward lunge exercise. Which of the following home care strategies should the personal trainer recommend to this client during the first 48 hours after the incident?

   A. Warm whirlpool with range of motion exercises for the ankle
   B. Rest, ice, compression, and elevation of the ankle
   C. Apply heat to the ankle, then passively stretch the calf
   D. Apply ice to the ankle, then actively stretch the calf

Scenario 3 (questions 34–35)

A 30-year-old woman has learned that she is six weeks pregnant. Although she has been running and doing resistance training on a consistent basis for three years, she does not know what exercise program to follow during her pregnancy. Her doctor has stated that she does not have any medical contraindications to exercise, so she hires a personal trainer to revise her program and monitor her workouts.

34. The day after the client signed a contract with a health club and a personal trainer, she slips and falls on the sidewalk leading up to the building and is injured. Which of the following is the MOST liable for her injury?

    A. The client
    B. The health club
    C. The personal trainer
    D. The health club and the personal trainer

35. All of the following should be part of the Emergency Plan of the client's fitness facility EXCEPT

    A. all policies and procedures should be written down.
    B. all facility members should sign a form stating that they will follow the plan.
    C. all emergency agencies and their phone numbers should be posted.
    D. all duties of each staff member should be described.

36. A personal trainer was asked by her client to help design a home gym. Which of the following recommendations should be made concerning the use of mirrors on the walls?

A. Mount them only on the wall opposite the main entrance.

B. Position the bottom edge a minimum of 20 inches (51 cm) off the floor.

C. Limit the height to the eye level of the tallest person to use the gym.

D. Place them on walls at least 2 feet (61 cm) away from the nearest equipment.

37. Which of the following describes how staff rehearsal of the facility emergency plan should be implemented in a fitness facility?

I. Regularly
II. Irregularly
III. Announced
IV. Unannounced
   A. I, II, and III only
   B. I, II, and IV only
   C. I, III, and IV only
   D. II, III, and IV only

38. While loading a bar for the squat exercise in a fitness facility, a client drops a 45-pound (20-kg) weight plate on his foot. The client is in significant pain and is unable to stand on that foot. The personal trainer should

A. contact the facility's staff.

B. direct the client to go home and put ice on the foot.

C. touch different areas of the foot to check for sensation and pain.

D. remove the shoe and perform an injury evaluation for broken bones.

Scenario 4 (questions 39–40)

An individual wants to add an exercise room to his house, so he hires a personal trainer as a consultant. The equipment for this room includes:

Dumbbells (5 to 60 pounds, in 5-pound increments)

Squat rack

400 pounds (182 kg) of weight plates

Multistation weight machine

Stereo, television, and DVD player

Adjustable utility bench

Olympic bar

Treadmill

Stationary bike

39. When designing the layout of the exercise room in this home facility, what is the minimum distance that should exist between the treadmill and the stationary bike?

A. 6 inches (15 cm)

B. 18 inches (46 cm)

C. 20 inches (51 cm)

D. 36 inches (91 cm)

40. The client asks his personal trainer to adjust the music volume during a workout. Meanwhile, the client begins his third set of the bench press exercise without a spotter, and drops the

bar on his chest, sustaining serious injuries. Is the personal trainer liable?

A. Yes, because the personal trainer showed willful and wanton conduct
B. No, because the client signed an informed consent form
C. Yes, because the personal trainer was negligent
D. No, because the client signed an assumption of risk form

Client Consultation and Assessment Answers

1. A. Before the fitness evaluation
2. D. III and IV only
3. B. II and IV only
4. D. Hypoglycemia
5. C. Bench press (maximum load divided by the client's body weight)
6. C. Replace foods to increase complex carbohydrate intake
7. C. At the initial client consultation meeting
8. D. Continual refusal to gain body weight
9. C. Completing the client–trainer agreement
10. B. During the health appraisal screening

Program Planning Answers

11. D. Negative punishment
12. B. Increased total blood hemoglobin levels
13. B. 160 pounds (73 kg)   15
14. A. Quarter squat
15. B. Hypertrophy
16. B. 70   45   20
17. D. Front squat
18. B. Back and hip flexibility
19. B. Cardiorespiratory
20. B. Increase carbohydrate intake

Techniques of Exercise Answers

21. B. Supporting the upper body with hands on the rails
22. D. Gluteus medius
23. B. Squat jump
24. A. When sitting on the ball, the client's hips and knees should be flexed to 90 degrees.
25. A. Minimizing amortization phase time
26. A. Minimize side-to-side arm swing
27. A. Rowing machine
28. C. Positive reinforcement
29. C. Exercise intensity   Exercise duration
30. B. Leg curl

Safety, Emergency Procedures, and Legal Issues Answers

31. B. II and III only
32. A. Increased exercise capacity during submaximal exercise
33. B. Rest, ice, compression, and elevation of the ankle
34. B. The health club
35. B. All facility members should sign a form stating that they will follow the plan.
36. B. Position the bottom edge a minimum of 20 inches (51 cm) off the floor.
37. C. I, III, and IV only
38. A. Contact the facility's staff.
39. B. 18 inches (46 cm)
40. C. Yes, because the personal trainer was negligent.

7 | # The International Fitness Professionals Association

The International Fitness Professionals Association (IFPA) is devoted to offering the highest-quality learning experiences to individuals who are aiming to improve their lifestyle and those who are aiming to improve the lifestyles of others.

IFPA educational opportunities provide only the most practical and scientifically based health and fitness information that can be directly applied to "real-life" experiences. It is with this dedication that the IFPA is committed to being the lifelong exercise and training resource for the entire fitness community. It is the organization's stated ultimate objective to train individuals to become leaders in the fitness industry in order to assist every person throughout the world in leading the health and fitness lifestyle.

Tell Me about the IFPA

Before the IFPA began in 1994, Dr. Jim Bell and many friends had identified a major problem in the fitness industry. The major certification organizations had fitness certifications that did an excellent job of meeting the academic criteria for what fitness professionals and specifically a certified personal fitness trainer should know, but they fell far short of the practical knowledge, skills, and abilities that a certified personal fitness trainer must know in order to conduct safe and effective personal fitness training sessions.

This team of subject matter experts (SMEs) put together the first Job Analysis Survey (JAS) in 1993 to determine the actual knowledge, skills, and abilities that certified personal fitness trainers needed in order to do their job with perfect execution. The JAS has been updated throughout the years and continues to be updated. The JAS is used by the IFPA Certification Commission to develop all IFPA exams and IFPA item banks (exam questions).

The IFPA-JAS is also used by the Fitness Institute of Technology to develop all IFPA course work. Since 1994, the Fitness Institute of Technology has developed over 60 IFPA certification courses, over 100 continuing education credit (CEC) courses, and multiple college degree programs (A.S., B.S., M.S., and Ph.D.) in medical-fitness training, sports and fitness training, and personal fitness training.

The SMEs involved in this meticulous development process use the highest level of effort, attention to detail, and both scientific knowledge and expert skills and abilities to always deliver the highest-level course work available in the world today.

The IFPA, the IFPA/ Fitness Institute of Technology faculty institutors, the founders of the IFPA, Dr. Jim Bell, and one hundred thousand and counting IFPA certified instructors and candidates continue to receive accolades because of the IFPA's mission of constantly striving for perfect execution and "Mastery of Our Craft." A few of those honors and evidence follow.

- Dr. Jim Bell was appointed to the Florida Governor's Council on the Obesity Epidemic.
- Dr. Jim Bell was appointed as co-chair of the American College of Anti-Aging Sports Medicine Professionals.
- Dr. Jim Bell was appointed as a board member of the American Academy of Anti-Aging Medicine.
- Dr. Jim Bell was twice selected as the lead speaker on fitness and nutrition at the U.S. Olympic and Pan American Coaches College, the first time in 1996 and the second time in 1998.
- The IFPA has certified 100,000 fitness professionals.
- The IFPA has 200,000 candidates in various levels of training preparing for certification.
- The IFPA has certified and trained the "stars" and leaders of the famous ESPN TV fitness programs, the International Federation of Body Builders (IFBB), the National Physique Committee (NPC), Olympic gold medal athletes and other Olympians, and world champion athletes and coaches in virtually every sport.
- The IFPA is the only fitness certification and continuing education credit course organization approved by the International Association of Continuing Education and Training (IACET) as an IACET CEC provider. IFPA courses offer both IFPA and IACET CECs for every program.

The IFPA Personal Fitness Trainer Certification Exam

The IFPA-JAS determined that the following six domains covered the critical knowledge, skills, and abilities needed by the certified PFT to carry out her job functions safely and effectively.

Their criticality was determined through psychometric analysis by the IFPA psychometrician to determine what percentage of questions would come from each domain.

The following domains and percentages are used to construct all IFPA examinations:

Domain	Percentage
Exercise physiology and anatomy	28%
Biomechanics and safety	25%
Program design	18%
Fitness testing and evaluation	12%
Nutrition	8%
Client consult and assessment	9%

Preparation Options

You may be passionate about fitness and wish to help people live the fitness lifestyle, but in order to do so you are going to need to make a living as a personal trainer. The IFPA offers various packages and supplemental products to both help educate you on the finer details of your craft and improve your readiness for passing the certification exam. These range in price from $25 practice exams to a $999 platinum package that includes a textbook, study guide, instructional video workshop with multiple DVDs, CD lectures, and CD-ROM programs, plus potential access to live workshops, with various levels in between, as the organization tries to meet both budget and study needs. At the core of the program is the $349 exam, featuring 105 multiple-choice questions, which is mailed directly to a proctor who will administer the test. The IFPA highly recommends that participants invest in some additional study resources not only to assist them with the material, but to ensure that they carry with them the knowledge contained within to their professional interactions.

Additional Fees and Services

The IFPA also makes available rush processing ($25), overnight shipping ($50), and a two-volume workbook ($89.95) with disk ($19.95). All exams are conducted online, so those applicants who wish to take a paper test will need to pay an additional fee ($25).

IFPA Sample Test Questions

(Answers can be found at the end of the chapter.)

1. The Karvonen formula is
    A. (220 – age) × 60 to 70%
    B. (220 – age – RHR) × (training %) + RHR
    C. (220 – age) × 60 to 80%
    D. (220 – age + RHR) × (50 to 65%) + RHR

2. The vastus medialis can be worked more intensely by
    A. leg extensions.
    B. leg extensions with "toe-out."
    C. leg extensions with "toe-in."
    D. lying leg curls.

3. A technique fault that the trainer should watch for while the athlete performs the bench press is
    A. bouncing at the bottom.

B. flaring the elbows to 45 degrees.

C. pausing at the bottom.

D. inhaling during the eccentric contraction.

4. Why is exhaling during physical exertion important?

A. Lowered blood pressure

B. Greater power

C. Greater repetitions

D. Alveoli protection

5. The weight training program that works agonist (one set) followed immediately by antagonist (one set) with no rest between the two is known as

A. a giant set.

B. a superset.

C. stripping.

D. an AG-AT set.

6. The type of weight training program in which the client achieves concentric failure, then is assisted by the trainer to achieve 2 to 4 more repetitions is referred to as

A. forced reps.

B. negative failure.

C. stripping.

D. power lifting.

7. _____ testing should never be performed immediately before muscular strength or muscular endurance testing.

A. Aerobic

B. 1 RM

C. Body composition

D. Circumference

8. The IFPA recommends that _____% of daily caloric intake be in the form of protein.

A. 12

B. 15

C. 20

D. 55

9. Excessive protein may stress what organ?

A. Heart

B. Kidney

C. Pancreas

D. Liver

10. Which of the following is a positive risk factor for coronary artery disease?

A. Men over 35 and women over 45

B. Blood pressure over 120/80

C. Total cholesterol > 200 mg/dl or HDL < 35 mg/dl

D. HDL > 60 mg/dl

IFPA Sample Test Answers

1. B. (220 – age – RHR) × (training %) + RHR
2. B. Leg extensions with "toe-out"
3. A. Bouncing at the bottom
4. D. Alveoli protection
5. B. A superset
6. A. Forced reps
7. A. Aerobic
8. C. 20
9. B. Kidney
10. C. Total cholesterol > 200 mg/dl or HDL < 35 mg/dl

CHAPTER 8

The National Academy of Sports Medicine

S ince 1987, the National Academy of Sports Medicine (NASM) has been a global leader in providing evidence-based certifications and advanced credentials to health and fitness professionals.

In addition to its NCCA-accredited Certified Personal Trainer (CPT) certification, NASM also offers a progressive career track with access to advanced specializations in performance enhancement (PES) and corrective exercise (CES), continuing education courses, and accredited bachelor's and master's degree programs.

The NASM educational continuum is designed to help today's health and fitness professionals enhance their careers while empowering their clients to live healthier lives. The organization has positioned itself as offering a premier science-based education with a focus on excellence, innovation, and results.

Tell Me about the History of the NASM

Focused primarily on sports medicine, nutrition, and the training of athletes, the NASM established its Certified Personal Trainer (NASM CPT) program in 1989, two years after its inception. By 1991, NASM certification had become a staple in health and fitness facilities, as a result of World Gym requiring all of its personal trainers to complete both an NASM CPT certification and a cardiopulmonary resuscitation (CPR) certification, also through NASM. Before the end of the century, NASM had joined its industry peers at the inaugural International Conference on Ethical Issues in Sports, and had also seen its certification become a requirement for all 24-Hour Fitness personal trainers.

In the twenty-first century, NASM's program has evolved, with the development of functional fitness (or kinetic chain assessment) to help identify asymmetries that lead to pain and even injury. The organization has also incorporated Dr. Michael Clark's Optimum Performance Training model (OPT) into its curriculum. Dr. Clark (DPT, MS, PT, PES, CES) is also NASM's CEO. He has rehabilitated, reconditioned, and trained hundreds of professional and amateur elite athletes, including a Major League Baseball Cy Young award winner, world champion figure skaters, NBA All-Stars, NBA Rookies of the Year, NBA Most Valuable Players, NFL All-Pros, the World's Strongest Man, national champions, Olympic gold medalists, and hall of fame athletes. He has also served as a physical therapist for the St. Lucia national team at the 2000 Sydney Olympics and Team USA Boxing at the 1996 Atlanta Olympics. In 2005, *Men's Health* magazine selected Clark as "Health and Fitness Visionary of the Year" for his role in shaping the future of the health and fitness industry. He is a noted lecturer and author, and is currently the team physical therapist to the NBA's Phoenix Suns and adjunct faculty for the master's of science in injury prevention and performance enhancement with the California University of Pennsylvania.

The profile of NASM's program has expanded over the last decade as well. The organization has established a foothold in the professional sports industry through its work with both the Suns and the Tennessee Titans. NASM's expertise was reinforced when it was selected as the "top visionary company to shape the future of fitness" by *Men's Health* magazine. Over 90 percent of National Basketball Association (NBA) athletic trainers have earned NASM CPT, Performance Enhancement Specialist (NASM PES), or Corrective Exercise Specialist (NASM CES) credentials. The program has gone on to earn international accreditation by the Registry of Exercise Professionals, and in 2008 it received further accreditation by the Commission on Dietetic Registration.

NASM has also taken to twenty-first-century media by instituting an e-learning center, allowing candidates to manage and complete their courses online. It also launched NASM PRO (nasmpro.com) in 2008, a Web-based business system for health and fitness professionals that provides access to a variety of resources, products, and revenue opportunities for personal trainers. NASM's partner company, NASM PRO, is now the Health and Fitness Provider Network (HFPN).

More recently, NASM was named a Military Friendly School by Military.com in 2009 for offering convenient online learning; special pricing for veterans, members of the military, and their families; and flexible testing schedules for soldiers who are called for active duty.

NASM Alliances Overview

NASM establishes strategic partnerships with best-in-class organizations whose technology, products, values, and vision complement its stated mission to deliver evidence-based health and fitness solutions that empower individuals to lead healthier lives. NASM strategic partners demonstrate a deep commitment to health and fitness, and are guided by core values that fit with NASM's research, development, and educational goals.

NASM's affiliations with leading higher-education institutions nationwide underscore NASM's commitment to providing the most cutting-edge educational curricula available. In fact, many of NASM's academic partners have incorporated NASM methods and materials into their accredited academic programs. Through NASM's academic partnerships, health and fitness professionals are invited to enrich their careers through a myriad of opportunities in higher education. NASM has also associated itself with many corporations and industry leaders to continually enhance its products and services while setting a benchmark for the health and fitness industry. Some of its alliances include

Arizona School of Health Sciences, at A. T. Still University–Mesa. Home of the world's first osteopathic medical school, the Kirksville College of Osteopathic Medicine, A. T. Still University is at the forefront of defining whole-person health care. In 2006, NASM and the Arizona School of Health Sciences at A. T. Still University (ATSU) launched a new online master of science degree in human movement.

California University of Pennsylvania. California University of Pennsylvania (CUP), a comprehensive regional institution of higher education and a member of the Pennsylvania State System of Higher Education, is a diverse caring and scholarly learning community dedicated to excellence in the liberal arts, science and technology, and professional studies that is devoted to building character and careers, broadly defined. NASM joined forces with CUP in 2005, producing an accelerated 12-month Web-based master of science degree in exercise science and health promotion.

University of North Carolina at Chapel Hill. Chartered in 1789, the University of North Carolina at Chapel Hill (UNC) was the first public university in the United States and the only one to graduate students in the eighteenth century. In 2007, the NASM Research Institute at the University of North Carolina at Chapel Hill was established.

dotFIT Worldwide. Founded in 2008 by a seasoned team of leading fitness industry visionaries, dotFIT Worldwide is rapidly becoming the worldwide leader in personalized holistic health and fitness solutions. NASM joined forces with dotFIT Worldwide in 2009 to unveil dotFIT.com—a complete online nutrition, fitness, and support platform.

Premier Training International. In 2009, Premier Training International joined forces with Performance Training Solutions (PTS) and NASM. The combination of Premier Training International and PTS creates one of the world's largest, most innovative, results-based health and fitness training providers.

National Basketball Athletic Trainers Association. In 2007, NASM signed an agreement with the National Basketball Athletic Trainers Association (NBATA) that established NASM as the official provider of sports education for the organization. NASM develops and markets instructional programs in consultation with the NBATA while serving as a resource to each NBA team's medical staff. Learn more at www.nbata.com.

Tell Me about Optimum Performance Training

Many training programs are based on the experiences and goals of body-builders, coaches, and athletes. As a result, much of what has found its way to the public has not been designed to meet the needs of our increasingly deconditioned and injury-prone society.

NASM's Optimum Performance Training method is a research-based, comprehensive training program that provides results that are specific to individual needs and goals. OPT incorporates multiple types of training—flexibility, cardiorespiratory, core, balance, reactive, speed, agility, quickness, and strength—into every program, improving all biomotor abilities while building high levels of functional strength, neuromuscular efficiency, and dynamic flexibility.

Assessment

At the center of the OPT method is assessment. All programs are designed based on a comprehensive and individualized kinetic chain assessment. This head-to-toe fitness and performance evaluation assesses an individual's strengths and weaknesses in the areas of posture, movement, strength, flexibility, and athletic performance.

Individualized Program Design

The OPT method provides an easy-to-use system for exercise selection based on the client's needs, abilities, and goals. The endless choices of exercises and the unique progressions keep every program fun, dynamic, and, most important, successful.

The following progression of success represents the various stages of the revolutionary OPT method.

1. *Stabilization endurance training* should be used for beginner clients who may have muscle imbalances or lack postural control and stability. This phase is crucial for all individuals, no matter what their goals, as it prepares them for the higher demands of training seen in Phases 2 through 5. Although this phase is the first phase of training in the OPT model, it will also be important to cycle back through this phase of training between periods of higher-intensity training seen in Phases 2 through 5. This will allow for proper recovery and maintenance of high levels of stability that will ensure optimal strength and/or power adaptations. This phase of training focuses on

   - Increasing stability
   - Muscular endurance
   - Improving flexibility
   - Increasing the neuromuscular efficiency of the core musculature
   - Improving intermuscular and intramuscular coordination

   The primary focus when progressing in this phase is on increasing the proprioception (controlled instability) of the exercises, rather than just the load.

2. *Strength endurance training* is a hybrid form of training that promotes increased stabilization endurance, hypertrophy, and strength. This form of training entails the use of superset techniques, where a more stable exercise (such as a bench press) is immediately followed by a stabilization exercise with similar biomechanical motions (such as a standing cable chest press). Therefore, for every set of an exercise/body part performed according to the acute variables, there are actually two exercises or two sets being performed. High amounts of volume can be generated in this phase of training.

3. *Hypertrophy training* is specific for the adaptation of maximal muscle growth, focusing on high levels of volume with minimal rest periods to force cellular changes that result in an overall increase in muscle.

4. *Maximal strength training* focuses on increasing the load placed upon the tissues of the body. Maximal intensity improves

    ■ Recruitment of more motor units
    ■ Rate of force production
    ■ Motor unit synchronization

    Maximal strength training has also been shown to help increase the benefits of the forms of power training used in Phase 5.

5. *Power training* focuses on both high force and velocity to increase power. This is accomplished by supersetting a

strength exercise with a power exercise for each body part (such as performing a barbell bench press superset with a medicine ball chest pass).

The NASM CPT Exam

The NASM Certified Personal Trainer exam consists of 120 questions, 20 of which are research questions. Research questions help the NASM develop fair and statistically valid examinations. Research questions are not counted for or against you, and you will not be advised as to which questions are the research questions.

NASM CPT Eligibility

To become an NASM CPT, candidates must meet the following eligibility requirements:

- Be at least 18 years of age.
- Have paid their NASM exam enrollment fees in full.
- Have current emergency cardiac care (CPR) and automated external defibrillator (AED) certification.

The NASM CPT Exam Enrollment Process

You can register for the exam by calling PSI/LaserGrade at (800) 211-2754 (in the United States and Canada) or Schroeder Measurement Technologies (SMT)/IsoQuality Testing (international) to confirm a date, time, and location for your exam. To find a PSI/LaserGrade location near you, visit www.lasergrade.com. You will be eligible to schedule your exam three business days after enrollment with the NASM.

Bring to the testing center a valid, current photo ID and CPR and AED certification from one of the following:

- American Heart Association
- American Red Cross
- American Safety and Health Institute
- St. John Ambulance
- Emergency Medical Technician

Upon completion of the exam, you will be given a score of pass or fail. To protect the integrity of the exam, test questions and answers will not be available following the test.

If you pass the exam, you will be able to print a temporary certificate from your member page after three to five business days. An official certificate will be mailed to you within four weeks of your passing the exam. If you do not pass the exam, you can call NASM-BOC three or more business days after taking the exam to purchase a retest. The retest fee is $99 and allows you an additional 120 days to take the exam. If you need to reschedule your exam appointment, you must call PSI/LaserGrade at (800) 211-2754 with more than 24 hours' notice or you will be charged a $50 late cancellation fee. If you do not show up for an exam appointment, you will be charged a $150 no-show fee.

Study Materials

Study materials available for the NASM CPT include an official textbook, a study guide, a DVD, an iPod video, an MP3 audio, and an Intro to Personal Fitness Training Course. There are also online learning modules via the Internet, in addition to practice exams and Webinar coaching series.

Live Workshops

The NASM also offers live personal training workshops designed to help applicants prepare for their Certified Personal Trainer exam, and also enhance their overall knowledge or develop a specialty. The workshops are two days each, with emphasis on assessment, exercise techniques, and exercise strategies. The Personal Fitness Training Live Workshop provides great hands-on experience for both those who are new to the field and veteran Certified Personal Trainers, while the Corrective Exercise Live Workshop offers excellent preparation for the NASM CES exam with a live instructor, and the Sports Performance Live Workshop provides the same for the NASM PES exam.

Tell Me about NASM's Other Educational Programs

The NASM CPT exam is the primary focus of this book, but in deciding which organization is right for you, it is worthwhile for you to know of and about the continuing education process, as well as other programs offered.

CPT Recertification

The purpose of the recertification program is to ensure that qualified professionals maintain entry-level guidelines by participating in approved continuing education programs. Continuing education programs are intended to promote continued competence, development of knowledge and skills, and enhancement of professional skills and judgment beyond the levels required for entry-level practice. Continuing education activities must focus on increasing knowledge, skills, and abilities as defined in the Job Analysis Study, 1st edition (2004).

To support NASM's commitment to protecting health and safety, the NASM CPT credential must be recertified every two years. This ensures that NASM CPT professionals are current with the best-practice guidelines and the specific knowledge, skills, and abilities described in the most recent Job Analysis Study.

To recertify, first visit www.nasm.org/Recertify. You must complete the NASM CPT recertification application or the CEU petition application for courses that are not recognized by the NASM BOC. Include with your application documentation of continuing education courses (e.g., copies of CEU certificates of completion). A total of 2.0 NASM-approved CEUs are required for the CPT and CGT. Also include a copy of the front and back of your adult CPR and AED certification (online CPR and AED certifications are not accepted) and the recertification fee of $99 (NASM will charge an additional $30 late fee if the application is up to three months late).

Mail all items prior to your certification expiration date to

NASM-BOC
26632 Agoura Rd.
Calabasas, CA 91302

NASM CPT Continuing Education Units Options

Moving forward on a successful career path is a natural with NASM. NASM builds skilled professionals by providing purpose-focused continuing education units (CEUs) that provide the knowledge and ability to achieve consistent results.

Every NASM certification requires recertification and the completion of a certain number of CEUs within a two-year period. NASM offers more than 20 personal training continuing education courses from which to choose.

Performance Enhancement Specialist (PES) Advanced Specialization

An elite training program for fitness and enhanced athletic performance, the NASM PES certification is designed for athletic trainers, chiropractors, physical therapists, coaches, and other sports professionals who want to work with athletes at all levels, from the secondary education and university tier to professional and Olympic-level athletes.

The NASM PES helps professionals learn cutting-edge performance assessment techniques and sport-specific program design. Scientifically valid, the NASM PES program provides evidence-based applications that achieve remarkable results with top professional athletes and weekend warriors alike. The NASM PES is the highest-level advanced qualification in the industry. It is the definitive training program for fitness and professional athletic performance.

Corrective Exercise Specialist (CES) Advanced Specialization

The NASM CES advanced specialization was developed in response to the growing need for professionals with the ability to assist clients who are experiencing musculoskeletal impairments, muscle imbalances, or rehabilitation concerns.

The NASM CES provides the advanced knowledge, skills, and abilities to work successfully with clients who are suffering from musculoskeletal impairments, imbalances, or post-rehabilitation concerns. By gaining advanced injury prevention and recovery knowledge, professionals place themselves among the elite in the industry.

The NASM CES not only provides professionals with cutting-edge, scientifically valid education, but provides applicable corrective exercise techniques and programming using the proprietary OPT model. The NASM CES certification integrates the science and solutions for optimal injury prevention and recovery success.

NASM CPT Sample Test

(Answers can be found at the end of the chapter.)

The Basics of Human Behavior and Psychology

1. An example of a vision question would be:
   A. Who are your role models?
   B. Have you ever been injured?
   C. What cardio exercises do you most enjoy?
   D. What are your daily consumption habits?

2. How much more likely to make successful life changes are individuals who are certain about what they want to accomplish than those who are less certain?

   A. 2 times more likely
   B. 4 times more likely

C. 6 times more likely

D. 8 times more likely

The Basics of Human Movement

3. The kinetic chain consists of

   A. the muscular, skeletal, and nervous systems.

   B. the skeletal, cardiac, and respiratory systems.

   C. the digestive, cardiac, and nervous systems.

   D. the muscular, respiratory, and digestive systems.

4. What structures are responsible for sensing distortions of body tissue?

   A. Chemoreceptors

   B. Mechanoreceptors

   C. Photoreceptors

   D. Peripheral nerves

The Basics of Training Assessment, Testing, and Workout Design

5. A proprioceptively enriched environment challenges which of the following?

   A. Maximum strength

   B. Speed, agility, and quickness

   C. Internal balance and stabilization

   D. Maximum cardiac output

6. The Optimum Performance Training (OPT) model is broken into which three building blocks?

   A. Stabilization, strength, and power
   B. Strength, endurance, and power
   C. Strength, cardiorespiratory, and nutrition
   D. Fat loss, strength, and hypertrophy

The Basics of Nutrition and Supplementation

7. Which fatty acids are considered to have favorable effects on blood lipid profiles and may play a role in the treatment and prevention of heart disease, hypertension, arthritis, and cancer?

   A. Saturated fatty acids
   B. Trans-fatty acids
   C. Monounsaturated and polyunsaturated fatty acids
   D. Chylomicrons

8. Which of the following bioenergetic pathways PRIMARILY break down carbohydrates to rapidly produce ATP?

   A. ATP-CP
   B. Glycolysis
   C. Oxidative
   D. Aerobic

The Basics of Safety, Rehabilitation, and Injury Prevention

9. Which of the following provides the health and fitness profes-
    sional with ongoing information to modify and progress a
    client through an integrated training program?

    A. PAR-Q
    B. Liability release
    C. Fitness assessments
    D. Body mass index

10. What form of flexibility applies gentle force to an adhesion
    "knot," altering the elastic muscle fibers from a bundled posi-
    tion into straighter alignment with the direction of the muscle
    and/or fascia?

    A. Static stretching
    B. Functional flexibility
    C. Self-myofascial release
    D. Active-isolated stretching

The Basics of Personal and Professional Success

11. Personal training has become one of the _____ professions in
    the country.
    A. least academic
    B. fastest-growing

C. lowest-paid

D. steadily declining

12. The acronym R.E.A.D. stands for

A. rapport, effective, accurate, decision.

B. relationship, empathy, accountable, demands.

C. rapport, empathy, assessment, development.

D. rapport, effective, available, development.

NASM Sample Test Answers

1. A. Who are your role models?
2. C. 6 times more likely
3. A. Muscular, skeletal, and nervous systems
4. B. Mechanoreceptors
5. C. Internal balance and stabilization
6. A. Stabilization, strength, and power
7. C. Monounsaturated and polyunsaturated fatty acids
8. B. Glycolysis
9. C. Fitness assessments
10. C. Self-myofascial release
11. B. Fastest-growing
12. C. Rapport, empathy, assessment, development

PART 2

BEYOND CERTIFICATION

Each of the certification organizations, as an important part of its curriculum, offers you strategies, tips, and advice to help you succeed once you get your certification.

Over the years, I've observed many real-world business lessons that I'd like to share with you as well. These tips and practices can save you lots of time, frustration, and money. If you're a certified trainer or thinking of becoming one, getting certified is only the beginning; you have to learn to deal with businesses and people in the real world.

In this section you will learn

- How to navigate around mistakes that new trainers commonly make, and how to raise your credibility by steering your clients away from the most common trainee misconceptions
- Effective workout routines, variations, and other tips to keep your clients satisfied and coming back for future sessions
- How to get smart about the business of training

CHAPTER **9** | # Avoiding Common Mistakes

You only have so much time available for work and play, and making good use of time makes our lives that much more enjoyable.

When it comes to making mistakes, the older we become and the wiser we get, the more we'd like to think that we can avoid them. I wish this were always true, but week after week, trainers and the people who use them keep falling into the same traps and bad practices.

So let's shake things up.

Let's take a look at some of the most common mistakes that both personal trainers and those who use them make and see if we can't change a few things to put our bodies, lives, and finances on a happier road that gives us more of the things we want and less of the things we don't want.

Personal Trainer Mistakes

Charging Too Much

One of the fastest ways to lose clients or have trouble finding them in the first place is by charging too much. For many people, using a personal trainer is a luxury, not a necessity. When the economy is tough and people are uncertain about their jobs and their investments, they tighten their belts and watch the "don't-need-to-use-right-now" expenses.

Having said that, regardless of what the state of the economy may be at any given time, there are people who will gladly pay top money for a trainer with a track record of proven results.

So how do you know how much to charge? If you're just starting out, look at the rates of the lowest-priced trainers in your area and price your services slightly higher.

Think of human nature: When people get bids for services, whether those services are for their home, their business, or whatever, more often than not they tend to throw out the lowest and highest bids and choose the one in the middle. Try that. Then, as your experience, expertise, results, and reputation begin to grow, consider upping your rates to reflect the increased demand for your services and your time.

Charging Too Little

The flip side of charging too much is charging too little. And yes, you can charge too little, with the result being that people will be wary of doing business with you.

People want quality, and for many people, the bad taste of poor quality remains long after the sweetness of the low price they paid is gone.

Value is all about perception, and if you can give your clients good results and the kind of service they will be happy with, then don't hesitate to price your services at least at current market rates, or even slightly above.

People want to feel good about what they spend their money on, and changing their bodies and their lives at a price they can afford is an irresistible offer that few will want to refuse.

Designing the Wrong Programs

I've seen trainers who've either read the latest research, attended recent seminars, or spoken to a so-called expert and come back to the gym all fired up and ready to try this gold mine of new information and knowledge on their clients. The trouble is, many times, it's not what those clients need or want.

Or a trainer may have established the programs, workouts, and strategies that he likes to use, and rarely deviate from them—regardless of the unique dynamics of a client.

The problem is that one size doesn't fit all when it comes to people and exercise programs or mental and nutritional approaches. The good trainers know this, and the lazy trainers couldn't care less.

Take the time to really get to know each of your clients. Make it your business to learn who they are, where they come from, their background and history, why they've come to see you, and what they are willing to commit to, because as a personal trainer, *this is your business*. You need to know where your clients want to go if you're going to help them get there.

Take the time to design a comprehensive custom program for each client. You want to not only get your clients the physical results they seek, but have them feeling fantastic while following your guidance and looking forward to each workout.

Choosing the Wrong Clients to Train

The fact that you are a certified trainer doesn't mean that you can or should agree to train every possible client who comes to you. Just as each person is different, each personal trainer has her own personality and strengths that will ideally fit some people, but not others. Your job is to know which people you can work best with and which ones are best trained by someone else.

Giving Less than 100 Percent Attention during the Training Session

People who use trainers say that one of the things that annoys them most is when their trainer is off in another world when he's supposed to be training them.

I see this often.

A client will be doing an exercise, and the trainer will get a cell phone call or text message. Or he'll start talking to someone in the gym—other than the client—while the client is right in the middle of a set. Or the trainer will be daydreaming and looking off in another direction rather than focusing on the client. If I were paying someone good money to train me for 30 or 60 minutes, and he wasn't giving me his full and undivided attention, unless there was a good reason for it, that would be the last training session I'd book with that trainer and the last dollar I'd send his way.

The best trainers I've seen are those who are locked into what they're clients are saying and doing throughout the entire workout. It's as if that client, for those 30 or 60 minutes, is the most important person and the only thing in that trainer's life—and the client knows it.

Hey, just remember that you're not the only personal trainer in town, but if you treat your clients like they're the only one in your world, you'll be the one trainer in town they won't want to leave.

Plateauing Results because of Ineffective Training Methods

If the client is giving you 100 percent effort each workout, then there are really two main reasons for results reaching a plateau: laziness and lack of knowledge. Take your pick.

Many trainers make the mistake of keeping their clients on the same type of training program or workout for too long. When the results begin to taper off and plateau, they blame the client first, rather than looking at themselves as the reason for the client's lack of improvement.

Give people a reason to look forward to seeing and paying you. Inspire them to keep coming to the gym to work out. Change their workouts regularly. Keep them fresh and new. Don't let your clients and their bodies get so used to what's going to happen again this week (the same things that happened last week and the one before it) that they stop coming to you altogether.

Creating a Monetary Dependence on a Core Group of Clients instead of Being Hungry for New Ones

Once you've struggled through the lean and tough times when you're just starting out and trying to get clients, and you reach the point where you have enough of them to make a good living, it can be easy to think that this core group of clients will be with you for a long time.

Some of them might be.

Others, however, even if you've been bringing them great results, will one day decide that they no longer want you to train them. People will always be flowing into and out of your life, and that's just the way it is.

As a trainer, your living is dependent on people coming into your life and wanting you to train them. The smart strategy is to always stay hungry and on the lookout for potential new clients—regardless of how successful you become.

Lack of Interest in Education and New Ideas and Methods

The person who thinks she knows it all when it comes to training, nutrition, the body, and people usually doesn't; more often than not, she is someone who has stopped growing. Here's a news flash: Your education doesn't stop once you get your college degree or become a certified trainer. That's when it really should begin.

Many times, our ego gets in the way of our either learning new things or listening to new ideas, and then applying them to our lives. The most successful businesspeople and trainers I know all share one thing: a hunger to know more, be more, and do more with their lives.

Keep your mind open to any and every new idea. Then put it through your "let-me-see-if-this-works" test. If it does and you like it, then keep it—until a new and better idea arrives to replace it.

Once you've got a great new idea and you'd like to begin putting it into practice in your business, speak to your clients about it. Find those for whom the idea would be a perfect fit, then try it and see what happens.

Not Operating Your Business Like a Business

Many people become trainers because they love working out and want to help people—and that's terrific. People gravitate toward those who are passionate and love what they do. Yet, even for the most passionate and successful trainers, unless they run their training business like a business, there could be problems ahead, and chances are they won't experience the kind of success they could.

So how do you run your personal training business like a business? Here are a few tips:

- Set up your business as an LLC (limited liability company) or an S corporation. This gives you a "corporate umbrella" that can protect your personal assets from things that can happen in your business. Talk to your attorney and CPA to determine which entity is best for you.
- Get the right kind of insurance. You need to be protected in case anything happens to your clients while they are being trained by you. Talk to your insurance agent to determine which type of insurance and the amount of coverage you need to be fully protected.
- Take care of all payment details in advance. There should be a meeting of the minds between you and your clients as to what your rate is and how and when they are expected to pay it before you begin training them.
- Keep good records. Find a good CPA and then determine which method works best for you when it comes to bookkeeping for your business income, deposits, expenses, and so on.
- Find a good bank. There are lots of banks to choose from. Find a bank and bankers who know you, like you, understand your business, and want to help you.
- Be a good communicator. You want to return calls, e-mails, text messages, and any communication you receive as quickly as possible (however, not while you're training a client!). If you're too busy, are going to be out of town, or don't e-mail or return calls frequently throughout the day, then forward your messages and pay someone to get back quickly to those who send them. You can then personally follow up as soon as it's possible for you to do so.

Choosing the Wrong Environment to Work and Train In

Some health clubs and gyms have such a good vibe about them that you look forward to arriving there. Others are just the pits and have such low energy that you can't seem to get your workout finished quickly enough or get out of there soon enough. If that's the way a place makes *you* feel, just think what your clients must be thinking and feeling!

Different clients respond best to certain environments, and you need to choose the best place to train them, even if it means paying an extra few dollars in facility use fees to train there. If it's the place your clients like best, then do it. Your number one goal is to get your clients great results and keep them happy. They'll thank you for it by coming back to you for next week's workouts.

Client Mistakes

Now let's talk about the mistakes many personal training clients make. Once you know their mistakes, you can better answer their questions and deal with any concerns they may have. Not only will you help keep them from making these mistakes, which is always a good thing, but you'll also build your own credibility, which will lift your personal training business to greater success.

They've Paid Too Much

You want to get what you pay for, right? So do your prospective clients, and the perception is that higher quality just costs more.

That's not always true.

There are some personal trainers who charge big hourly rates, but aren't known for getting big results. There are others who have a reputation for achieving fabulous results for their clients, but who don't charge overly high rates.

It's all about what each would-be trainee is looking for, how good he feels about the person who's training him, and what he feels most comfortable in paying.

A big factor that determines personal training rates is geography. Using a trainer in Manhattan, New York, is going to cost significantly more than using one in Manhattan, Kansas. It costs more to do business in New York City than it does in the Midwest, and people who live in New York City know it and will expect to pay more.

To make sure that price isn't the only factor your prospects use in making their decision (knowing that those same potential customers have cheaper options available), give them references to contact. Confidently advise them to listen to the experiences that others have had while working with you. Invite them to meet you face to face (if they haven't done so already) and try one workout together to make sure you're a good fit. If the test drive feels good, they'll move forward and begin enjoying the ride. And if you've followed along, they'll feel good that they're getting their money's worth.

They've Paid Too Little

Client prospects who are always on the lookout for the cheapest trainer they can find have probably already been burned by bad service. Just as paying too much doesn't guarantee anything except having spent too much, more often than not, when someone always tries to pay too little, she's become accustomed to getting what she's paid for—too little. It's up to you as a trainer and salesperson to sell her on the value of your service.

A caveat: Trainers who are just starting out and need clients can use their situation to their advantage if they're up front about it. Pitch yourself as being armed with a head full of new knowledge and passion to share, but needing clients to share it with. You're not some devalued poor-man's-consolation trainer; you're someone who is willing to cut a great deal with the right client who is willing to trust you.

By "cutting a deal," you're saying to yourself and your customers that generally your time would be more expensive, but the circumstances (you're just starting out) have created a special opportunity. When the circumstances change, you can confidently adjust as new business walks through your door.

And here's a big bonus: The trust and loyalty you reward your first clients with translates into instant marketing for your business. Their word of mouth will be more effective in generating new clients than most other initiatives you can think of. Your first clients, who have all benefited from your enthusiasm and your commitment to them (along with the extra attention you may have paid them while you had the time to do so), are valuable enough to your business that it may be worth it to keep their "introductory rate" even years after you've become the next hot thing with a ton of other clients who are gladly paying you far more money.

They Keep Going Despite a Lack of Results

When it comes to workouts and fitness, if clients are not getting the results they want, but they keep going to and paying the same personal trainer, then eventually they're going to ask themselves why.

People have lots of choices when it comes to whom they'll pay to train them, and just as it's up to you as a trainer to personalize and mix up their program, it's also in your best interest to recognize a potential client who has burned out on a bad trainer.

When you pick up on that frustration while you're interviewing a would-be new client, you need to sell strategy and results to set the client at ease. You're talking with someone who is actively seeking help, and it's up to you to show him how you're going to give it to him and what he can realistically expect. Give him testimonials. Let him watch you in action. Show him the bodies of those you've trained, and if he likes what he sees and hears, he'll make the switch and won't think twice about doing so.

They've Become Psychologically Dependent

A good friend of mine, Rachel McLish (the first Ms. Olympia), once said about trainers and those who go to them, "If you trust someone else too much for your physiology, be careful that you don't trust them too much for your psychology."

So what is Rachel saying here?

It can be good to push someone to get into shape, but only up to a point. Many times, I've seen people essentially give up their own personal power and give it to a trainer whom they want to take care of everything for them. That whole "I don't want to work out without you" or "I can't do this by myself" mindset becomes a debilitating crutch that can not only cost them a lot of money (for their physical/mental therapist), but keep them from trusting themselves and growing.

It's the client's body, her dreams, and her goals that are hanging in the balance, and it's in your best interest to teach her how to apply the knowledge that you're sharing. Build up your clients mentally by reminding them that they are the "doers" who are doing the heavy lifting (literally). The stronger they are mentally, the more potential they'll realize they have, and the more faith and loyalty they'll place in you to help them reach their goals.

When a client does feel that she's outgrown your sessions together, she becomes the type of success story that reputations are built upon—a walking, talking, interactive billboard for your services.

They've Got Unrealistic Expectations

Lots of people start and stop exercising because they get frustrated and lose interest. Much of that frustration comes from having unrealistic goals and expectations—that is, wanting too much too quickly.

A trainer can do only so much in a certain period of time. A person who is out of shape and hasn't exercised for a long time isn't going to get in fabulous shape in 30 days or less, regardless of what someone tells him or what he may expect.

Yes, there are some trainers who put their own monetary interests ahead of their clients' and have no problems telling people what they want to hear. Thankfully, trainers of this kind are very few in number.

The majority of personal trainers know their clients and know what those clients can realistically expect from them, and they won't sugarcoat what needs to happen and how long it needs to happen before the client's goals can be reached. If you're honest with your clients and give them realistic expectations, they'll reward you with continued business as they meet those expectations.

They Lack Discipline

While it's true that it's not how long someone trains, but what she does *when* she trains that makes the difference, it's also true that what she does outside the gym greatly affects the results she gets inside the gym.

If a client misses workouts or eats improperly, then her results are going to be hit-or-miss, and minimal at best. Consistent training and watching the diet are the cumulative things that get the body in shape, make weight loss possible, and put strength goals within reach.

That said, who do you think a client is going to look at first when she fails to achieve the results she envisioned—you or herself? It is up to you to position your workout sessions in the gym as simply one of the numbers in the combination that unlocks a client's fitness success. A good diet, plenty of rest, keeping stress levels low, and the right mindset are the other numbers that clients need if they are to make their fitness and health a reality—and if you don't emphasize and remind them of this, their failure could be yours as well.

They Lack Training Intensity

Just because people come to the gym and work out four or more days a week doesn't mean that they will get good results. In sports and in fitness, the name of the game is intensity. The more focused the effort, the better the results.

There's an old in-the-gym exercise maxim that goes: You can either train long or train effectively, but rarely can you do both.

Now, there are sport-specific training methods that do require lots of endurance and longer training sessions. However, for most people who simply want to look and feel better, effective workouts don't need to be long-drawn-out workouts. Turbocharge your clients' stagnant workouts and give them better results by reducing workout volume and time by 50 percent and increasing their training intensity by 70 percent or more.

They Get Distracted by the Wrong Workouts

The media are always heralding the latest fad routine, and your clients are listening. Don't make the mistake of letting them believe that the over-the-top workout they've read about or seen someone else doing is the one they need as well. For every popular program that gets results, there are a dozen that serve only to distract your clients from the plan you've mapped out for them to reach their goals. At the same time, you can't be dismissive of new ideas (for your own good as well as your clients'). It's up to you to do the homework and give your clients the answers that random blogs and filler news pieces won't.

A great trainer knows his clients' body type, their experience and ability level, the goals they have set, and great ways to get them where they want to go. Your clients trust you (that's why they pay you for every workout), so you need to be their go-to source for answers.

When your client comes to you with that new workout he'd like to try, use the knowledge you have at your disposal to identify the best elements of it. Then suggest that he try one portion of the new workout so that you can observe what happens. If he likes it and it produces a good result, then consider adding another element or so to the routine.

This is a smart approach.

It allows you to introduce new things without abandoning what's worked thus far, protecting your client's investment and further raising your credibility. Every time your client is able to tell others what "my trainer said," following up with a sound, rational explanation of what is and isn't effective, his loyalty is rewarded and your reputation swells.

The key to long-term great results is very straightforward. Know your client's body, and then train it with the right exercises and workouts in the ways to which it responds best.

10 | Training Different Body Types

Of all the things I've written about over the years, one that has struck a nerve with people is how they should train their body type and custom-design their workouts and lifestyles for it. As I tell people, it's rare for any of us to be purely one body type; rather, we're a blend of body types, with one of those types being the dominant one. Just look at your clients and you'll see just how true this is.

You know that working out makes you feel and look good. When you hit the weights regularly, your body changes, and for the better. You also know that the basic exercises will help you get on the road to fitness success, but soon you'll reach a point where knowing your body type and how it responds to training will take on new importance—especially if you're training other people.

The three basic body types are:

- *Ectomorph*, characterized by long arms and legs; short upper torso; long, narrow feet and hands; narrow chest and shoulders; very little fat storage; and long, thin muscles
- *Mesomorph*, characterized by a large chest, long torso, great strength, and solid musculature
- *Endomorph*, characterized by soft musculature, short neck, round face, wide hips, and an inclination toward heavy fat storage

Again, as a rule, nobody is just one particular body type. We tend to be a combination. But each of us leans toward being one of the three types, and knowing how these different body types respond to training and diet helps your clients reach their fitness and bodybuilding goals more quickly.

Understanding each client's body type and the specific training and nutritional demands for growth that this type entails presents new challenges for you. These challenges require that you have a solid game plan to be successful in helping your clients reach their training goals.

Training and Nutrition for the Ectomorph: When Putting On Size Is Hard to Do

The person who is an ectomorph tends to be thin, lean, and lanky. Typically, an ectomorph will have a short upper torso; long arms and legs; narrow chest, shoulders, feet, and hands; and long, thin muscles.

Ectomorphs are leaders in the expedition for muscle size and weight. However hopeless it may seem for ectomorphs to gain slabs of beef or become a champion bodybuilder, they shouldn't lose hope. Champions like three-time Mr. Olympia Frank Zane and many other great body-builders were at one time all ectomorphs.

The Importance of Intensity

If your client is an ectomorph, building muscle mass can be quite a challenge indeed. Ectomorphs tend to be lean, and putting on size may seem to take forever if they're not following a solid game plan. However, with proper guidelines, you can help them get to their fitness and bodybuilding goals quickly. These tips will help:

- Do the basic exercises that emphasize power movements for building mass. Exercises like squats, dead lifts, presses, chins, rows, barbell curls, and the like are excellent mass builders.
- Keep the reps in the six to eight range and sets in the eight to twelve range. Be sure that they give their body enough rest between sets so that they can continue to lift heavy, with good form, to induce muscle-fiber stimulation for growth.
- The training goal should be less volume and more intensity. Train no more than three days per week in order to give the body sufficient time for recuperation, repair, and growth. The Monday-Wednesday-Friday workout schedule is ideal.

Nutrition is a big factor in gaining weight and muscle mass for ectomorphs. They need to take in extra calories throughout the day. Weight gain powders and protein drinks complement their overall solid nutritional plan while boosting their caloric intake. Limit outside activities in order to save their energy for building muscle mass.

Here are some other training and nutrition tips that are sure to help the ectomorph in his muscle-building and strength-gaining goals.

Use Power Movements and Train Heavy; Skip the Isolation Work

The ectomorph needs to lift heavy weights to hit the deep muscle fibers that will make the body grow. Don't waste time on isolation or cable movements right now. If your client is an ectomorph, she should do the following:

- For legs: squats, stiff-legged dead lifts, donkey calf raises
- For chest: dumbbell or barbell incline presses
- For back: chin-ups; barbell, dumbbell, or T-bar rows
- For shoulders: dumbbell or barbell front presses
- For biceps: barbell or dumbbell curls
- For triceps: close-grip bench presses, dips, or lying EZ-bar french presses

Take Longer Rest Periods, and Get a Good Night's Sleep

Ectomorphs tend to train at a fast pace and would benefit greatly—both in recovery and in strength—if they slowed down. Intense training is the stimulus that creates muscle growth. Intensity can be accomplished in a number of ways, two of the best being lifting heavy and resting longer between sets, and training lighter with shorter rest time.

Because high-intensity workouts are a necessity to make the ectomorph grow, the focus should be on lifting heavier and taking longer rest periods between sets to ensure greater muscular recovery for maximum intensity and strength for each set.

Ectomorphs must also give their bodies adequate rest between workouts. The absolute *minimum* amount of rest that an ectomorph needs is 48 hours between workouts of the same body part. And they should never work a body part unless it has *fully* recovered from the previous workout. Because of their high metabolism, ectomorphs should get no less than 7½ hours (and preferably 8 to 9) of sleep every night.

The Nutrition Factor: Eat, Eat, Eat

Training is unquestionably an important element in the ectomorph's body-building success, but good nutrition is too! In fact, one of the biggest reasons ectomorphs have so many problems is that they eat too many of the wrong foods, eat too little of the good foods, and don't eat often enough.

To simplify things, structure their diet in the following way:

1. Eat five to seven small meals daily.
2. Increase your daily protein intake to 1 to 1.5 grams of protein per pound of body weight.
3. Aim to get your protein intake to no less than 35 percent of your daily total caloric intake.
4. Have a protein shake 90 minutes *before bedtime*.
5. Make carbs 45 percent of daily dietary intake.
6. Increase your daily intake of fibrous carbs (cauliflower, broccoli) while limiting your intake of simple sugars (fruits, honey).
7. Keep the fat intake to roughly 20 percent of your daily dietary intake.
8. Eat slower-burning glycemic index foods such as beans, sweet corn, lentils, yams, peas, nonfat dairy products, porridge, oats, and pasta.

9. Supplement with a good multivitamin/mineral.
10. Drink lots of water throughout the day—at least 80 ounces.

Keep Stress Levels Low through Meditation

Many ectomorphs are high-strung individuals. They're usually amped up and on the go. For such individuals, stress can be a problem because it affects progress in the gym by producing cortisol, a catabolic (yes, the opposite of anabolic) hormone.

Ectomorphs should practice slowing things down and relaxing. Try slowing their pace and having them take at least 10 minutes a day to be off alone and away from people and noise. In those 10 minutes, have them lie down or sit relaxed, close their eyes, inhale through their mouth and exhale through their nose, and slowly and softly repeat the words "calm," "serenity," and "tranquil."

Have them feel their muscles relax and become heavy as if concrete weights were attached to them. Tell them to imagine that all stress is leaving their body and dissipating in the air. Nothing can bother them. They are in control.

Minimize Outside Activities—Don't Get Run-Down!

Because most ectomorphs have metabolisms as fast as a greyhound's, their bodies tend to burn the food they eat very quickly. Many ecto-morphs I've talked to and worked with complain that they can't put on size. There's a good reason for this: They don't eat enough of the right foods, they don't train correctly, and they engage in too much activity.

If your client is an ectomorph and his big goal is to pack on more size and strength, he should minimize all activities other than weight training. The goal is to make sure that his body uses all the nutrients he consumes so that he can recover and grow from his workouts.

If a client must be involved in other physically demanding activities, be sure that he takes in extra calories—above those that he is taking in for bodybuilding—and gets plenty of rest. By following these guidelines, your client's weight- and strength-gaining problems will be history.

Training and Nutrition for the Mesomorph: Born for Bodybuilding

You can say that mesomorphs are natural bodybuilders. The ability to put on muscle is not really a problem for the mesomorph, although it still takes effort, intensity, and perseverance. Mesomorphs, like endomorphs and ectomorphs, benefit from proper training and nutritional guidelines. Here are a few:

- Using a combination of heavy power movements like squats, dead lifts, rows, and presses, along with shaping movements such as laterals, pressdowns, dumbbell curls, and extensions, can give the mesomorph better muscle quality, proportion, and symmetry.
- Mesomorphs respond well to fairly long workouts (up to 80 minutes) and shorter rests between sets (no longer than 45 to 60 seconds). Staying within the range of 6 to 10 sets and 6 to 12 reps works well for the mesomorph.
- Working out four days a week, such as two-on, one-off, seems to give the mesomorph's body enough workout frequency and stimulation for growth.
- A balanced diet is generally good enough to allow the mesomorph to pack on muscle mass. There is no need for her to overload her

system with massive amounts of protein or carbs. She should eat sensibly and keep the body fat to an acceptable level.

- Whatever your client's predominate body type is, remember that she is still a combination of all three body types.

The Easy Gainer Workout

Blessed be the mesomorphs—those genetically gifted people who seem to gain muscle just by thinking about it. Well, not quite that easily, but mesomorphs are bodybuilding's fastest muscle gainers. Yet, despite their propensity to accumulate slabs of muscle in a hurry, mesomorphs need the right training and nutrition program to make the best gains possible.

The Mesomorph's Special Training Needs

The male mesomorph is typically muscular and naturally strong, with a long torso and a big, full chest. The female mesomorph is stronger and more muscular and often more athletic than other women (or girls). A mesomorph's strength can increase very quickly, as can his or her muscular size, especially on the right program.

A mesomorph responds well to training that involves heavy, quick movements along with shaping exercises. The more varied the exercise program, the better the results.

Take quads, for example. After a good warm-up, a mesomorph could begin with a great mass movement like squats, followed by hack squats or leg presses, and finishing with a shaping movement like leg extensions.

For hamstrings, the mesomorph might begin with stiff-legged dead lifts, followed by a shaping movement such as standing leg curls. For calves, the first movement might be heavy standing calf raises followed by high-rep toe raises with light weight on the leg press.

The More Variables, the Better

Mesomorphs should make repeated changes in the variables involved in working out—that is, the number of sets, reps, and exercises; length of training sessions and rest; number of training days; amount of weight used; and various exercise angles.

They should also vary their training intensity. A combination of three to four weeks of intense training followed by one to two weeks of lower-intensity training seems to promote growth and strength, and prevent training burnout.

Fuel to Build High-Quality Muscle Mass

Mesomorphs grow best when they get plenty of protein—at least 1 gram per pound of body weight daily—and keep their carb intake moderately high. The surprising thing about the majority of the mesomorphs I know is that they can follow a diet with more than 20 percent of calories from fat (still far less than the typical American diet) and it actually helps them gain mass and strength!

In fact, many mesomorphs can boost their strength levels simply by increasing their fat and protein intake moderately. Strange as it may sound, a tablespoon or two of peanut butter a day can do some amazing things for a mesomorph.

A mesomorph typically will make strength and muscle gains by keeping his body weight relatively steady, looking to increase muscle mass only gradually. The days of bulking up by 20 or 30 pounds and then cutting down are over for mesomorphs who want to gain the greatest amount of *quality* lean tissue. In fact, for all individuals, quality muscle size can be gained much more quickly when body fat levels are held under about 16 percent for men (about 22 percent for women).

The Aerobic Factor: Keeping the Fat Off

If building muscle is the goal, intense cardio work such as running should be kept to a minimum. Running long distances can be counterproductive. Many mesomorphs can lose lean muscle tissue quickly if they run more than two miles three times weekly.

Some mesomorphs have found wind sprints to be an excellent way to condition and build the hamstrings, quads, and calves, while aerobically conditioning the cardiovascular system.

If running isn't for your client, try having her use the stair stepper, stationary bike, racquet sports, jump rope, or treadmill or having her hike. Just make sure she doesn't overdo it. Three times per week, 25 to 30 minutes per session (5-minute warm-up, 15 to 20 minutes in your target heart range, 5-minute cool-down) will work well for burning fat.

Of course, your clients probably won't be able to do that when it comes to jumping rope. So, have them jump for 3 to 12 minutes and rest only long enough to keep their heart rate in the target range. In fact, that's the key to doing all their cardiovascular exercise. To find the target heart rate range per minute, subtract their age from 220 and multiply by 0.6 and 0.8. Your answers represent the range in which they should be exercising aerobically.

The Overmotivation Factor

Since mesomorphs can make outstanding gains quickly, some individuals may be inclined to push themselves to the limit. Training intensely is great, but doing too much too quickly can lead to overtraining and injury.

Over the years, the sport of bodybuilding has been rife with genetically gifted mesomorphs with the potential for phenomenal growth and strength. But because of overenthusiasm, they either burned out, injured themselves, or lost the motivation to continue training.

If your client is a mesomorph, he should consider himself fortunate. But he needs to be sensible with his training and nutrition. Those two factors will help him reach his fitness goals and potential.

Have him stay committed to his training. Show him how his body type responds to various training methods, sets, and reps. Structure his training to his body type needs, and you will lead him to success.

Training and Nutrition for the Endomorph— High Reps, High Sets

Building muscle mass is generally easier if you're an endomorph. However, keeping fat levels low may be more of a challenge. Generally, the endomorph responds well to high-set (12 to 15), high-rep (12 to 20) training that allows for only brief rest between sets. Endomorphs respond well to training no more than four or five days per week, as with a two-on, one-off program.

Aerobic training using stationary bikes, treadmills, stair climbers, and other such equipment for at least 20 to 30 minutes per workout should be included in their program. Keeping the caloric intake of protein, carbs, and fats to restricted levels is important, but not at the expense of going below their daily nutritional requirements for muscle repair and growth.

Training for the Endomorph

One of the questions asked most by fitness enthusiasts is, "How should I train?" As you can imagine, coming up with one answer is a challenging task. We all have different body types, goals, levels of experience, motivation, training time, nutritional needs and habits, and other factors.

Since what works best for one person may not work for another, I will present some practical, in-depth training advice for the endomorph—the kind of body that tends to be heavyset.

And while many of the exercises I discuss for the endomorph (or any other body type) will work for any build, it's *how* you do them that can make all the difference with regard to your body type.

The Endomorph Training Philosophy: Emphasis on Intensity and Aerobics

Endomorphs typically have a higher than normal percentage of body fat. On the plus side, many endomorphs are blessed with a big and wide bone structure. However, weight gains come easily, and losing body fat is much more difficult.

Many times, the weight that endomorphs gain stays right where they don't want it—on the abs, waist, and buttocks. As endomorphs begin weight training and bodybuilding, they tend to gain size—much of it muscle—fairly quickly. However, it often remains hidden under layers of fat. Ironically, an endomorph's body can be hard as a rock, yet achieving a good degree of definition always seems just out of reach.

Many endomorphs, because of their advantageous bone size and ability to put on muscle quickly, train with heavy weights and low reps. Often this is a mistake. An endomorph should train with moderate poundage, high intensity, minimal rest between sets, and more frequent workouts. The goal is to amp up the metabolism, make the muscle burn, and carve new cuts and definition.

Another *very* important training element is cardiovascular fitness. Far too many endomorphs simply do weight training and nothing else. That's another big mistake.

An endomorph will never achieve the degree of leanness she desires unless she has a good diet and trains her cardiovascular system at least three times per week. Excellent cardiovascular workout choices include brisk walking, the stair-stepper machine, stationary or regular bike, racquet sports, hiking, and walking on the treadmill.

Have your endomorph clients do their cardiovascular training in the target heart zone, a range that is dependent on their age. To compute their range per minute, subtract their age from 220 and multiply that number by 0.6 and 0.7 (note the different range for the endomorph from the mesomorph). After a 5-minute warm-up, have them exercise in their target heart zone for 15 to 20 minutes, then cool down for 3 to 5 minutes.

The Endomorph Workout

As always, let's keep the workouts fun. That means changing the training program regularly—like every second or third workout. From there, follow these tips for success:

- Take three to five exercises that work well for each body part and use those as the pool of exercises to choose from for each workout.
- Choose two or three different exercises for each body part from the pool of exercises for each workout.
- Do one basic movement (i.e., incline dumbbell press for chest) and one or two isolation movements (i.e., dumbbell flies, pec, dec, or cable crossovers).
- Decrease their rest time between sets to no more than 60 seconds.
- Keep their reps in the 9 to 12 range for the upper body and the 12 to 25 range for legs and calves.
- Each workout, vary the rest times, reps, sets, and weight. Keep their body constantly off guard.
- Train abdominals at the beginning of the workout.
- Do no more than eight sets per body part.
- Work out on a split-training system. For example, on Monday work chest and arms, on Tuesday work legs, and on Wednesday work back and shoulders.
- Thursday is a day off from weight training, then have them repeat the training schedule starting on Friday.

The Role of the Brain

One of the most important training tips for the endomorph to keep in mind is training intensity. The endomorph must constantly keep his training intensity high. Make the body work harder by working smarter using the guidelines just given. Keep the workouts fresh and exciting, and don't allow yourself to fall into a rut. Do something different each workout. It will make a huge difference.

CHAPTER 11 | Working Your Clients: Exercise and Environment

Having personal training clients is a great thing. You're helping to change someone's life for the better, and you just never know what a difference doing so will make in the world. It's that "ripple effect" of one positive action creating numerous positive actions because of it.

For a personal trainer, the goal is to both get clients and keep clients by giving them great results and making them happy. You know that from a pure equipment standpoint, a well-equipped gym offers you and your clients the greatest variety of tools that you can use to get them in shape and accomplish their goals. Some people you'll train will love free weights and wouldn't be caught training on a machine. Others think machines are safer, are more comfortable, and provide the best workout. I think a combination of the two produces amazingly effective results. In this chapter, we're going to discuss the many variations you can explore with your clients using both machines and free weights.

But what if you have a client who is uncomfortable with the idea of going to a gym or health club right now? He wants you to train him and help him. He just wants you to do it in an environment where he'll feel most comfortable. We're also going to discuss a training option that may prove mutually beneficial in creating a workout environment where both you and your clients can thrive.

Entering their home.

Regardless of the facility or the equipment, it's your job to bring a challenging program to your clients that is both created with their goals in mind and appropriate to their body type. In doing so, you must also take into account the realities of their daily lives and customize their journey to give them the best chance to see it through—exploring your options when it comes to specific exercises and an environment that will help lead you (and them) there.

Great Machine Exercises

For years, there's been a debate about which is better: machines or free weights. Trainers say that clients ask about it often. Depending on whom you talk to, what you read, and what camp you may find yourself in, they both have their pros and cons.

Look in any gym and you're likely to see rows of machines. Some are fancy, some not, but they're all designed to make working out better and more effective. And even many homes have mini-gyms nowadays.

But as good as machines are—and some of them are excellent—they're still based on making the body work through a certain range of motion in a fixed groove or track. And that can be where one of the biggest limitations of machine training will be found. Barbells and dumbbells don't have the kinds of limitations that machines do.

The other limitation is real weight versus machine weight. Because machines have pulleys, cams, cables, and the like, much of the weight your client thinks she's lifting has been reduced.

For example, chances are that an 80-pound dumbbell french press is going to feel different from an 80-pound cable french press with the cable traveling through one, two, or more pulleys. Much different.

We've seen and heard stories of the athlete who can power up 350 pounds on the machine bench press, only to turn blue in the face when he's sitting under 275 pounds with a barbell over his body. So, always keep that in mind when using machine training with your clients.

The other is the question of whether machine training is right for a client's body. In other words, if he's got long arms, short arms, long legs, short legs, or any other extreme extremity, he may find that machines are designed to accommodate and work optimally with a certain size body, and his may not be it.

Clients may also discover, as many people do, that finding a machine that feels good for their body and works it in the fullest range of motion (if that's how they like to train) can be quite difficult.

Now, having said all that, machines do have their place in a workout program, and they can be quite effective if they're used in the right way. I'm going to share with you some great machine exercises and body position nuances that will help you keep your client on machines as long as she (and you) wants, giving her results that she can be very happy with in the process.

Multistation Machine

- *Low-pulley cable curl (biceps).* Keep this in mind: The closer clients are to the low pulley, the harder the initial pull and subsequent tension throughout the movement. Likewise, if they stand away from the pulley, the same weight will feel lighter.

- *High-pulley cable pressdown (triceps).* Regardless of what bar or rope they use, position clients close enough to the weight stack so that the cable travels in a direct vertical line (not at an angle) throughout the range of motion. This will work the triceps harder.
- *Low-pulley upright row (traps).* Have clients keep their body positioned far enough away from the low pulley so that the angle between the machine weight stack and the cable forms a V as they pull. Use nonstop reps of 15 or more and descending sets for a great pump.
- *High/low-pulley cable lateral raise (shoulders).* Clients can also try this movement with the cable behind their back. For rear delts, have them use both high pulleys and pull across their body.

Multistation with High/Low Cross Pulleys

- *Cable crossover (chest).* For a different feel, have clients do their reps leaning forward at the waist and in line with the weight stacks, almost mimicking those most-muscular poses you see bodybuilders perform.
- *Cable fly (chest).* To really feel it, position the bench—incline, flat, or decline—so that the client's arms and hands and the cable are in a direct line with the center of the weight stacks.

Pull-Down Machine

- *Front and back pull-down.* To contract the back better, have clients use a reverse grip. Keep their backs slightly arched and their elbows far behind them in the bottom position.

- *High-pulley cable curl (biceps)*. Clients will lie on a flat bench with their head directly underneath a high cable and pulley while holding a short bar attached to the high pulley. Keep their upper arms at 90 degrees, and curl the bar toward their face. Have them slowly return to the fully extended position. Go for high reps.

- *Low-pulley preacher curl (biceps)*. Keep clients' elbows close and their grip wide. Always have them fully extend their arms before doing their next rep.

- *Lying leg curl (hamstrings)*. Clients will rest their forearms on the bench under them to elevate their upper body. As they curl their legs, have them try to drive their hips into the bench, which will help isolate the hamstrings as well as protect the lower back.

- *Seated leg curl (hamstrings)*. For a greater stretch, clients should lean slightly forward throughout the entire movement.

- *Standing leg curl (hamstrings)*. Have clients keep their torsos upright. Encourage them to go all the way up and squeeze each rep, then bring the leg all the way until they get a full stretch. Use minimal rest between sets.

- *Leg extension*. Be sure your client's body is positioned back far enough so that the area where his hamstrings and calves meet is touching the seat. Have him go for full extension and lock-out at the top of the exercise along with a full quad stretch by having his feet come as far as possible under the seat at the bottom of the exercise. Nonstop high reps work great.

- *Seated calf raise (calves)*. Go for a full calf stretch with the heel all the way down at the bottom. Clients should lean forward so that their upper body is over their knees to feel a greater calf burn.

Power Rack/Smith Machine

Let's first talk about the Smith machine. This machine has two vertical guide rods, and a barbell that's attached to them travels up and down in a fixed groove.

The barbell goes only straight up and straight down. But even with that, some great exercises can be done on the Smith machine, such as presses, squats, shrugs, rows, and lunges. Here are a few pointers for each.

- *Presses (incline, decline for chest, and seated/standing press for shoulders).* Have clients keep their elbows wide and pointed away from their upper body. Instruct them to keep them straight up and down, resisting the inclination to pivot them forward or backward. Experiment with non-lock-out high-rep sets and lead them to different hand spacings every few reps within the same set to demonstrate how differently they will feel it.

- *Squat (quads).* The Smith machine is especially good for wide-stance squats with feet pointed out to work the inner thighs. Clients should place their heels 6 to 12 inches in front of their upper body; be sure to point out the difference in sensation from squatting with heels directly below. For wide-stance squats, have them keep their legs and feet directly under the bar. For all squats, make sure their knees travel in a direct line over their middle toes, but no further.

- *Lunges (quads, hamstrings, glutes).* Clients will stand under the bar as if they were doing a squat. Have them lower the bar, and as they do, they will extend one leg, bending down the other directly in a straight line below their body with the bent leg's foot behind the body. Instruct them that it's "Just as if you were kneeling down, only with one leg that's doing the work in front of you." Push for high reps of 15 to 30 for each leg before switching legs.

- *Row (back)*. This is a good exercise to introduce your clients to strip sets. After they do six reps, take some weight off each side, then have them do four more reps. Repeat this one more time and push them to rep out until they reach failure.

Leg Press

If you have access to a leg press machine, great; here are a few exercises and variations that you can work your clients with.

- *Adductor press (inner thighs)*. Instruct clients to keep their legs perpendicular to the foot platform and use a wide stance, turning their feet out 20 to 30 degrees. Have them lower the weight and bring their legs out to the sides of their body, then push the weight back up by squeezing the inner thigh muscles.
- *Vertical leg press (inner thighs/quads/hamstrings)*. When leading your clients through regular leg presses, have them experiment with foot placement (always keep the knees traveling in a straight line over the toes). I like using full-range reps, though other people like using short-range (lowering the weight about 4 to 10 inches) reps. To squeeze extra contractions out of them, have them lock their knees and rock back on their heels as they push to full extension, allowing their toes to rise off the platform.

Quick Tips for Better Results with Free Weights

Okay, time for some quick tips that will help take any exercise and make it even better. As much as these tips are geared toward free weights, as discussed earlier, some of them can be applied to machines as well.

I've always been a big believer that it's not about using a lot of weight as much as it is about feeling the exercise work—making the muscle burn and pump. That's why I love using different angles, hand placements, and positions. I'll teach you some of them to show to your clients.

Changing Your Grip

If you or your client takes a wide grip on a barbell and does a bench press rep, it's going to be felt in the outer pecs. However, when you bring the hands closer together, you'll feel it in the inner chest and triceps.

Remember what I told you about having clients change their grip from wide to close when they work their backs? It's the same exercise, but they'll feel it in different parts of the muscles they've been working simply by changing their hand grip and spacing.

Changing the Angle

A great example I like to use is working the biceps. If your clients do curls standing up with their arms close to their body, they'll tend to feel it more in the upper biceps. Try telling them to squat down, with their upper arms and elbows resting on top of their legs, and then do a curl. With their arms at more of an angle, they'll feel it more in the lower biceps.

Changing Foot Position

When working legs and calves, there are essentially three ways to change foot position to target different aspects of the calf and thigh muscles:

1. If you have your clients point their feet straight, it tends to work the entire calf.

2. If you have them turn their feet outward, they'll be directing their work to the inner calves.

3. If you have them turn their feet inward, they'll be focusing their work on the outer calves.

For legs, the same rules apply. Feet positioned straight ahead will tend to hit the entire thigh area more evenly. Feet turned out will direct the work to the inner thighs, and feet turned slightly inward will tend to shift the work to the outer thighs.

To help prevent injury, on all leg work, be sure to keep the knee always in a line with the toes.

Changing Elbow Position

I know you probably wouldn't think so, but simply moving a client's elbows up, down, into the body, or away from it can affect what the exercise will target, and what she'll feel as a result.

Let's take the dumbbell kickback. Most people will do this exercise with their working upper arm either close to their body or hanging down below their body. Wrong!

The trick is to keep the upper arm close to the body, but make it come up above the upper body. Try this yourself and see. Do a dumbbell triceps kickback; the higher you raise the dumbbell above your body, the tougher this exercise will get. You can do the same with the pressdown simply by moving your elbows in close to your body or away from your body.

How about biceps? Like dumbbell curls? Good; you'll like them better if you simply change elbow positions: do them wide or close, elbows forward or elbows back.

You can do the same with barbell curls, cable curls, and the list just goes on. The most important thing to do is experiment and find your best elbow, foot, angle, and grip positions. They'll help turn good exercises into great ones!

The Home Trainer

Home is the place your clients know and feel best. As a result, clients are more likely to be receptive to your ideas and suggestions for exercise and nutrition when you can train them in comfortable surroundings.

For a personal trainer, the goal is to get clients, then keep those clients by giving them great results and making them happy. So, how can you make the case to any client who may be sitting on the fence about having you train him because he's not crazy about joining a gym right now?

I've got some good suggestions that I'd like you to share with them that can help you get and keep those clients who want to be home-trained.

Let Them Know What They Can Expect

We're so used to people promising us the world, then being disappointed by the results. Tell your clients that you're not going to promise them anything except that you're going to give them the information and tips that can change their body if they'll only use them. Make the argument that you would like them to not expect any certain thing, but to be open to everything. This will help them experience results that are greater than their expectations and will help them stay motivated and looking forward to their next workout, and the next, and the next.

What They Need to Know

Let them know that they already have everything they'll need to achieve great results for a lifetime. Everything. If they've got a body, a good mind, and a desire and a will to take action, then they've got what they need.

In life, whether its having a great body or learning a new skill, let your clients know that it helps to ask lots of questions and learn as much as they can from anyone and everyone, then try out those things they've learned and see if they work for them.

In a very short time, your clients will quickly learn what works and what doesn't, and it's then that they start filling their own toolbox with the right tools that work and feel best for their body, their goals and dreams, and their life.

The Arguments for Home Training

You'll find that home training will be great for some of your clients for lots of reasons. In addition to giving you an overhead-free workplace, here are a few of the benefits you can describe to get them off the fence and into the back room:

- *You can train whenever you want and for as long as you want.*
  The reality is that a client doesn't need to train very long or very

often to get fabulous results. Let's say she's working out at a gym and running late, but her workout isn't finished.

- Well, that means that either "that's it" for her today or she'll have to come back to the gym later and finish her workout—which, if she's like most people, is just not going to happen.

- Working out at home easily solves that, since it's so easy for her to pick up where she left off—plus she won't have to get into the car and drive to the gym.

- *Home training is very convenient.* You can be to "your gym" in only seconds. Enough said!

- *Home training saves time.* By the time your client gets ready for a workout, gets in the car, fights traffic/delays, gets to the gym, and actually gets out on the gym floor ready to do his first exercise, there's a good chance that he'll have spent about 30 to 40 minutes. Add the time for him to work out, shower and get dressed, get back in his car, fight traffic/delays, and return home, and he can easily use up over two hours.

    Compare that to throwing on a pair of shorts or sweats and a T-shirt and walking a few steps in his house when he wants to exercise. He's looking at about three minutes, and that's if he's a slow dresser.

- *Home training is more comfortable.* How much more comfortable can you get than working out in the privacy of your home? Forget having to dress in fancy workout clothes like so many people do in gyms or being overly sensitive about how you look or what other people will think of you. Who cares? Remind clients that when they're working out at home, you're the only one there, and it's your job to train them, not judge them.

- *Home training is cheaper.* With many gym/health club memberships costing well over $300 a year, working out at home can be much cheaper. For the price of a barbell or a dumbbell set, remind clients that they could save hundreds of dollars just in the first year. And if all they want to do is nonweighted, bodyweight-only exercises, then they'll save even more.

  Now, add in how much money they save in gas and the biggest of all, their time, and they've got some powerful reasons to make their home a home gym.

- *Home training builds confidence and self-image.* One of the biggest fears that people have is thinking that they're either too fat, too out of shape, too skinny, or too something else to be seen working out in a public gym or health club. This fear keeps so many people from exercising and changing their bodies and lives for the better.

  When we all begin, we're all a little afraid of not knowing what to do, how we look, and what others think of us. For guys, it tends to be a fear of what other guys will think. Am I too weak? Too skinny? Too fat? Too out of shape? Do I look like a beginner? Am I doing the exercise right? Do I look confused?

  Similarly, for women, it tends to be what other women will think. Are my hips, thighs, butt, legs, abs too fat? Am I wearing the right clothes? How does my body look in them? I don't know anybody here, and it's making me uncomfortable. And, of course, the fears about being a beginner play a part.

  Explain to your would-be home-training clients that all these are only natural. With each workout, their confidence will grow. As their body begins to change and they start feeling better about themselves, their confidence will soar until they very quickly reach the point where it starts to feel really good being who they are, how they look, and in their own skin.

Home training can be just the confidence builder that many people need, since there's no one but the trainer there to see a client when she's just beginning. It also helps keep clients focused on their workouts and their goals, since they don't have to deal with all those fears about themselves and other people judging them that come into the back of their mind when they're at the gym.

Then, as their confidence builds each day with each workout, there's a great chance that those fears won't be a factor if they ever do want to go to a gym.

The Full Circle

Let your clients know (and this may surprise them) that many of the people who have great bodies, the kinds they might admire, actually started their training at home. Not only that, but while many of them started at home and eventually went to gyms and health clubs, many of those same people went full circle and came back to working out at home again. So let it be known that they can have the body and the health they want without ever having to leave the house.

It's so easy to look for answers to our lives outside of ourselves—as in thinking that one must train at a gym or health club, listen to the latest expert or guru, or try the latest workout craze. The reality is that anyone can look and feel great with a complex full of expensive equipment or with a minimalist room that houses nothing but hard work and dedication—it's all up to the individual. The equipment or the gym is only a means to an end; it's never the end result. These are things people might use to help them get to the end result that they may want (a great body), but by no means are they necessary for them to achieve that result. There are people all over the world who exercise with no equipment and don't eat the variety or quality of foods that we have in the United States, but they still achieve spectacular results. Just think of what your client is going to be able to achieve thanks to your knowledge and the tools at hand!

Get your clients to start thinking of what they're about to embark on as a journey that can make their body look and feel better. Others say they know the best way they must travel to do it, but tell them to stay focused. No one knows what your clients need more than they do, and only they can decide to give it to themselves—especially with your help!

Allow them the freedom to try things they might not have ever imagined possible. Such as looking and feeling great *without* going to a gym.

CHAPTER **12**

Getting Smart about Business and Building the Business of "You"

E ven though the subject is fitness, the decision makers, the gate-keepers, the promise makers, the clients, and the money givers are all people. Once you hit the streets to "do business" and interact with the dynamics of people in business—whether you send an e-mail, Twitter, IM, text, pick up the phone, send a fax or FedEx, or meet a client in the gym—the whole playing field completely changes, and if you want more success, you'd better know a few good rules.

They Never Told Me It Would Be Like This

Once they get certified, many trainers are surprised at just how much they need to bust their butts to find clients they can train. Don't get me wrong; there are *lots* of people out there right now who are looking to be trained, and who will happily pay great money for it, but they need to know about you. They need to know that you're around and looking for them. And then, once you've connected with them, you've got to close the deal and get them to say yes to trusting their bodies, their results, and their money to you.

Know Thyself (and Others!)

Have you ever asked yourself why you work out and love doing so? If you've got a good answer to that question, then you've found one of the many answers to why other people do it too. Truth be told, you and other people who work out (or want to) have a lot in common. It doesn't matter whether you started training to lose weight, gain weight, get stronger, become leaner, get over an injury, prevent an injury, or something else. All that matters is the end result—to change your life for the better in some way.

If you are to help every client, you have to achieve that end result— regardless of who a client is, the experience level she has, or the life story she has lived—and if you do so, you will have more clients, business, and money than you'll know what to do with.

The Flowchart of the Fitness Business and Life

Have you ever noticed how when your goal is achieved or you get great news, many other people also benefit as well?

You get your certification, and you're out at a party or talking to someone when the subject of fitness comes up. You tell him that you just got certified, and he tells you that's so weird, because he's been thinking of finding a trainer and getting back in shape.

It happens all the time.

The message is: You don't have to know all the answers or know every road you'll take to your goal beforehand. Stay open to the possibilities of what's out there, and let the natural flow of people and life find its way to you and yours.

You're going to enjoy the ride.

Okay, I Pick You!

One of the biggest mistakes that people make in business (and in their personal lives) is choosing the wrong people in their lives. Too often, the hangups of people with bad attitudes and ideas or overwhelming insecurities can become your handcuffs as their negativity seeps into your thinking and beliefs.

Start looking at your life like it's a major league pro team. The teams that win the biggest honors and enjoy the greatest success are those that have the best players and the best management. Pretend you're the owner of your own major league team, and with a careful eye, start choosing the best supporting cast of people who will empower you personally and professionally. You're looking to fill your roster with those who will protect and encourage you and who genuinely believe in you and your dreams.

With them, the sky will be your limit.

Make Yourself "Most Wanted"

You can have the most knowledge and the most certifications from all the best certification organizations there are, but if people don't connect with you and you aren't giving them results to brag about, then all you'll be is another "certified trainer."

Go the extra mile.

Make yourself stand out.

Do the things the others aren't doing, can't do, or won't do.

Create your own unique brand that people will know you for. All the greatest businesses do it, and there's no reason why you can't do it, too. Then, once you've created your brand and your unique way of doing things, refine it to perfection by the service you offer and the results you create.

Then get ready for your phone to start ringing off the hook.

The Mills Lane Expletive Fund

Some years ago, there was a pro boxing referee named Mills Lane. Years of military service had made him one tough cookie who no one wanted to mess with, and a memorable character for sure. He was short and bald, and he had a no BS attitude.

I remember an interview with him in which he talked about the ups and downs in his life—especially the financial pressures he had once faced. As someone who didn't like receiving orders and enjoyed being the one giving them, you can imagine that waiting for others (businesspeople) to make decisions that would affect his life didn't sit well with him.

That's when he decided to change things, he said. He vowed that he'd work hard, make as much money as he could, and then save and invest it.

Mills Lane said he called it his "F-You Money," because if anyone offered him a business deal or opportunity that sought to take advantage of him, his experience, or his talents unfairly, he could afford to tell them no and push them to come back with a better deal. If they didn't, he had plenty of money saved, and he could walk away without a regret.

That's a great lesson.

The world of business is full of ups and downs, good times and not so good times, lots of money coming in and hardly any dough arriving.

So protect yourself.

Start your own Mills Lane–style savings fund. It'll help you stay in control of your destiny and weather anything the world can throw at you.

The Natural Cycles of Surges

Throughout your fitness career, you're going to find that there will be times when your business is booming, and other times when things are kind of quiet. Don't let it worry you. It's simply the natural cycle of surges that people in all economies go through.

When times are good, people are working, home prices are rising, and folks have a little jingle in their pockets, they don't think twice about spending money on the "extras" in their lives, like a personal trainer. When times are tougher and the money doesn't jingle as much or as loudly, people naturally cut back on luxuries and focus on the necessities.

And that's when you have to turn their personal trainer from a luxury into a necessity. You do it by giving them such good results whenever they are with you that they don't want to be without your help. That's why even in bad times there are lots of personal trainers whose incomes and client base don't change, and even grow! People want to spend money on the things that make them feel good. Give them great results and service unlike anyone else's, and they'll keep spending that money with you.

The Power of Synch

One thing that frustrates people when it comes to business and dealing with people is that others rarely want to work on someone else's time frame. They have their own goals, objectives, and agendas, and if they have the money and you want to get some of it, then you need to learn how to make their time frame your time frame.

So, how do you do that?

Begin by creating lots of opportunities with many different people and businesses. You'll find that some of them will fall into place and happen very quickly, some will take a little longer, and a few will be long-term works in progress. Then constantly make adjustments to your future business plans by moving the various projects you have up and down, in order of importance and action, based on the daily and weekly feedback you receive. Whenever a current or future project is completed, then move all the others up the list and add new initiatives to take the place of any you finish.

Remember that life is exciting in proportion to the number of things you have to look forward to. When you have lots of projects going on, and others that will happen at some point in the near future, then you're in control of your destiny and are directing it toward a happy result.

Control the Worry Factor

In both your personal and your professional life, there'll be times when, despite your best efforts and hard work, things just won't seem to be happening and moving forward. For so long, we've been taught that it's only by "our" actions that we accomplish anything. But sometimes life has other plans.

That's when you need to relax, take a deep breath, and step back from what's going on in your life. It's the time to stop worrying and to be a little patient.

As a trainer, not only do your clients depend on you to bring them a depth of knowledge and understanding that will help them, but you are also their motivational coach for those 30 or 60 minutes that they are with you, and if you're worried about every little thing that someone says or does, then your clients will know it. Your body will be there, but your head and mind will be off in a whole different place.

There's an old saying that goes, "Ninety-nine percent of the things we worry about never happen and the other one percent that do are not even worth worrying about." Let go of the little things that have been bothering you and forget what's in the rearview mirror. All that matters is today and where you want to go tomorrow.

Make Failure a Trusted Friend

If you look at the history of men and women who achieved amazing things, you'll discover that at some point in their lives, the majority of them experienced many failures and setbacks. Instead of seeing these experiences as stopping points, they used them as valuable learning tools that became huge stepping-stones on their road to success. You can do the same.

When you're starting out, and even after you've been in business for a while, there may be times when you lose clients and business. When that happens, look closely at the reason why. Did another trainer or facility offer those clients something that you weren't offering? Was there something about your attitude and approach that turned a client off?

Be honest with yourself, get over your ego being temporarily hurt, and find the answers that will help smooth out the rough edges of your approach so that you can turn any seeming failure into a great success.

Finding the Trigger Points

While clients may come to you so that you can be their physical, sports, or nutrition teacher, they will also teach you the most valuable lesson a trainer can learn when it comes to dealing with people.

"Why?"

The best trainers have the skills to know what their clients need and why. They ask a lot of questions. They are terrific listeners to both verbal and nonverbal communication. They then create the perfect program that each client needs at that time in her life, knowing that at each workout, adjustments may need to be made that will keep their clients happy.

Nothing stays the same in this life of ours, and that holds true for any clients you may have, so just stay fluid and flexible, listen to what they need, and give it to them.

People Will Treat You the Way You've Trained Them to Treat You

Many of us see who we are through the eyes of other people. That is, we like to think that we know what they think of us, and we create our self-image based on what we imagine they think we are.

Sounds kind of crazy, doesn't it?

After all, we really have no idea how others truly view us, and even if we did take the time to find out (and most people don't because they are so busy thinking about everything else in their lives), we'd be surprised at how wrong are perceptions are.

Instead of spending so much of your priceless life and valuable time caring about what others think about you, simply be the person you imagine you'd like to be. Treat people with love and respect. Be a person of your word. Go the extra mile and give your clients more and better service and results than they expect. And fill your life with all those qualities that you like and that make you feel terrific.

You'll then be living the life you imagine, and what you imagine, you will soon become.

Be the Rabbit, Not the Fox

People are a funny bunch. You could have been the best trainer in your city for years with hardly anyone knowing about you, but if you do something that gets notoriety or come up with something that gets people talking, they'll flock to you.

People want to work with those who are successful. They want the best giving them the best. So, how do you stop chasing them and get them to start chasing you?

Start creating a buzz.

Put that crazy dream or idea you have about a new training system or workout to the test. No limits! All the most-popular diets and workouts started that way. Someone had a dream and told others that they had to try it and they did, and word of mouth spread like a wildfire and the phenomenon started.

You can do the same.

The New Fitness/New Dream Law of Resistance

So, let's talk a little more about what happens when you take your exercise, workout, or nutrition visionary ideas and test them on the world.

Once you test your new idea and you get the following reactions and responses, you'll know you're on to something good:

- "You're crazy."
- "It'll never work."
- "You're lucky."
- "You're a visionary."
- "You're the one I want to do business with."

Mentor Me Now

Some of the best and wisest time you'll ever spend in your life is those 10 minutes with someone who's already the area's top trainer or who has gone through the tough times you've been going through and become a success because of it. Being around them will change your life faster than a year of studying books.

You see, even the best trainers had to start somewhere, and each of them started at the bottom. But it was what they did and how they did it that got them to the top.

Take them to lunch, ask lots of questions, and then listen. Your life is about to be changed for the better because of it.

A Signed Deal Is Just the Beginning

You love working out and you love training people and helping them, and you'd probably do it for free if you could. But you've got your life to live, things you want to buy, and investments you want to make, so you need to get paid.

That's when you need to start thinking more like a businessperson and less like a trainer.

Come up with a system that works great for your clients and you, whereby each party knows what's expected of him and when. You make a commitment to train a client at certain times of the week, and he makes a commitment to you to be there and to compensate you for your time and expertise.

I suggest using a very simple one-page agreement for every client you have. Be sure to have an attorney draft it for you so that you are fully protected and your agreement is valid within the laws of your state and where you do business. The agreement should spell out what you will be giving the client, and the client agrees to engage the use of your services and pay you an agreed amount at a specified time and in a specified way. And be sure the agreement states that the client understands and agrees to not hold you (and your company) liable for any injury, and so on.

You've got better things to do with your life than chase down people all over town trying to get the money they owe you. Put everything in writing, protect yourself, and everyone will know the rules and be happy.

Always Remember: It's Just Business, Not a Marriage

Let's take this dealing with people in business thing one step further.

In your business life, you'll find that you need to deal with many people only once, others only a few times, and a select few (hopefully in a good way) longer.

Before long, you will get to the point where you'll be able to pick and choose the clients you want to work with, and that's when it's nothing but fun.

Until then, keep your mindset in the proper perspective by understanding that you're building your business and there will be all kinds of people who will cross your path who will help you do it. Keep the happiest people and experiences, and let go of the rest and wish them the best.

Be a 30-Second E-mailer

One of the nonfitness things you can do that will make you stand out is the quickness with which you respond to e-mails and questions. Some people make the mistake of thinking that if they get an e-mail, they'll get back to it and answer it perhaps a day or so (or longer) down the road.

Big mistake.

If someone took the valuable time out of her life to think about you and e-mail you, then show her the same respect and courtesy by taking the time to reply.

And the quicker you can do it, the better.

That shows those people that they are important to you and that getting back to them is a priority. They'll remember you for it, and when it comes to them scheduling another trainer session or choosing between you and someone else, you've just stacked the odds in favor of them making the call to you.

Say "Thank You," and Say It Often

Here's another great way to open doors and have people remember you: Say "thank you," and say it often.

People don't have to do business with you.

People don't have to call or e-mail you.

People have other options.

So make yourself memorable in a good way in their minds, by thanking them for any good words they tell you and any things they do for you—like using you as their trainer!

People want to feel loved, needed, and appreciated.

Telling them "thank you" is a great way to make them feel that way.

Tough Times Are Here Only for a Short Time

We all go through tough times. It's as if life uses those adversities and tough times to wake us up and teach us the valuable lessons we need at the time so that we can learn, grow, and move to the next higher level in our life's journey.

So, whenever the business ebbs or the tough times seem to arrive in bunches, step back and give yourself a breather and some perspective.

Tough times never last too long, and soon you'll be enjoying those happy times once again.

Do Not Be a Prisoner of Your Own Decisions

One of the things that will keep you fresh, current, and always growing in your personal and professional life is to be fluid. Always be open to changing anything and everything, and don't become a prisoner of your own decisions.

Many people do.

They'll think about doing something and finally decide to do it, but they will rarely adjust their plans or change things along the way. Then when success doesn't happen fast enough or they're not getting the results they've wanted, they become frustrated and blame the world—anyone and anything but themselves—for why things aren't happening.

Be different from that.

Make a decision and take an action, but if it isn't giving you the results you want, change it and keep changing things until it does.

It can be your training approach with clients. It can be taking all that textbook training knowledge and fine-tuning it for the "real world" you live and work in each day.

Whatever it is, wherever it is, whenever it is, change is good.

"You Jump through My Hoop and I'll Be Happy to Jump through Yours"

Many people make the mistake of being the nice guy or gal who'll bend over backward to help people in any way possible. All of that is well and good, if they return the favor. But for lots of people, those who give too freely of their time, talent, genius, and efforts are looked upon as a cheap commodity in the business marketplace and are unjustly undervalued by those who receive their help.

Hold yourself up to a higher standard.

Be kind to people, but let them earn your time and expertise. You are the one who has the skill, talent, and knowledge that will help them, and they need you. Don't give it away or sell yourself too cheaply.

It's Time for You to Become the Person behind the Plow, Not the Mule Pulling It

Lots of people go through their entire lives working for someone else and are totally happy. Others have the desire to do their own thing in their own way and start their own business. I think you know which group you belong to.

You may begin your career as a trainer by working for a health club. Many people do. Then, once you build a good clientele, you may decide to start your own personal training business and use that health club—and many others—as the place where you train your clients.

Regardless of whether you stay an employee or become the president of your own company, always remember that you control your destiny. You may work for a company, but only you can offer that club's clients the unique skills and abilities that can get them the kind of results that only you can bring them.

And if you've started your own business, focus your time, energy, and expertise on the things that pay you the greatest rewards and farm out as much of the rest as you can to others. The most successful CEOs all do this, and there's a good reason for it: Your time is better spent doing the things you're an expert at.

Time to Empty Your Cup

Every six to twelve months, take about 15 minutes and make an inventory of where you are and where you're going. Change, throw out, or revise your plans as needed.

This is also the time to take an inventory of the people in your life.

Keep the positive people and let go of those who are bringing you and your business down. No one says you have to keep the same ideas, clients, or other people in your life who are not bringing joy and happiness to it, so let your negative influences go.

The New You: Maverick, Pioneer, Fitness Success Extraordinaire

Ask 10 people how you should live your life and you'll get 10 different answers. It seems that lots of people who don't know you are out to convince you that they know exactly how you should be living the life you are living.

But let's get real.

No one knows you better than you know yourself. And you don't need anyone telling you what you should do and how you should do it.

Follow your own intuition and gut feeling. It rarely is wrong.

In fact, if you'll look back to the moments when you made decisions that didn't work out as planned, don't be at all surprised to find that those were the times when something inside of you knew better and told you not to proceed, but you didn't listen.

Never let another person's ideas, opinions, and conclusions become your reality unless you know deep down that you are in complete agreement with what they're saying.

Appendix

Contact Information

To learn more about any of the organizations featured in this book, you can contact them directly via e-mail, their Web sites, and social networks, as well as through traditional lines of communication.

NSCA

1885 Bob Johnson Drive, Colorado Springs, CO 80906
Phone: (719) 632-6722
Fax: (719) 632-6367
Toll-Free: (800) 815-6826

NSCA National Headquarters: nsca@nsca-lift.org
NSCA Certification: exams@nsca-lift.org

ISSA

1015 Mark Avenue
Carpinteria, CA 93013
(800) 892-4772
International call: (805) 745-8111
Fax: (805) 745-8119
www.issaonline.com or www.issaonline.edu

ACSM

Contact: www.acsm.org, (800) 486-5643

Street Address:
401 West Michigan Street
Indianapolis, IN 46202-3233

Mailing Address:
P.O. Box 1440
Indianapolis, IN 46206-1440

Telephone:
Monday–Friday, 8:00 am–4:30 pm (ET)
National Center (317) 637-9200

Fax:
(317) 634-7817

NCSF

www.ncsf.org
(800) 772-NCSF (6273)

NFPT

P.O. Box 4579
Lafayette, IN 47903
(800) 729-6378
Fax: (765) 471-7369
www.nfpt.com
nfpt@nfpt.com

IFPA

14509 University Point Place

Tampa, FL 33613

(813) 979-1925

(800) 785-1924

Fax: (813) 979-1958

www.ifpa-fitness.com

NASM

26632 Agoura Road

Calabasas, CA 91302

(800) 460-6276

Fax: (480) 656-3276

www.nasm.org

Follow NASM on:

www.facebook.com/PersonalTrainers

twitter.com/nasm

Index

Home training, 240–245
Human body, ix–x

I

IACET (International Association of Continuing Education and Training), 175
IFPA (*see* International Fitness Professionals Association)
IFPA certification exam, 175–180
    details of, 175–177
    sample test answers, 180
    sample test questions, 177–179
IHRSA (*see* International Health, Racquet, and Sportsclub Association)
Ineffective training methods, 207
Insurance, business, 209
Intensity of training, 215
    for ectomorphs, 219–220
    for endomorphs, 228–229
    for mesomorphs, 230
International Association of Continuing Education and Training (IACET), 175
International Association of Fire Chiefs, 65
International Association of Fire Fighters, 65
International Council on Active Aging, 65
International Fitness Professionals Association (IFPA), 173–175
    certification exam of (*see* IFPA certification exam)
    contact information for, 265
International Health, Racquet, and Sportsclub Association (IHRSA), 58–59, 130, 131
International Sports Sciences Association (ISSA), 121–141
    accreditation of programs, 122, 131
    on benefits of online education, 123–126
    certification programs of, 126
    Certified Fitness Trainer exam from (*see* ISSA Fitness Certification exam)
    contact information for, 263
    continuing education required by, 131

continuing education resources from, 128
    curriculum of, 122–123
    and NCCA accreditation, 131
    other programs of, 128
    philosophy of, 121–122
    support services from, 123, 127–129, 132
    teaching method of, 126–127
    unique advantages of, 130–131
Introductory rates, 212
Isolation work, for ectomorphs, 220
ISSA (*see* International Sports Sciences Association)
ISSA Certified Fitness Trainer (CFT) certification, 128
    continuing education requirements for, 131
    exam for (*see* ISSA Fitness Certification exam)
ISSA Certified Fitness Trainer course, 126
ISSA Fitness Certification exam, 126, 132–141
    sample test answers, 141
    sample test questions, 132–140
    study and testing options, 132
ISSA Fitness Therapy (FT) certification, 128
ISSA Specialist in Fitness for Older Adults (SFOA) certification, 128
ISSA Specialist in Fitness Nutrition (SPN) certification, 128
ISSA Specialist in Sports Conditioning (SSC) certification, 128
ISSA Youth Fitness Trainer (YFT) certification, 128

J

Job Analysis Survey (IFPA), 174

L

Lack of results, in training, 212–213
Lane, Mills, 250
Leg press machines, 237
Legislative Action Center (ACE), 62
Limited liability company (LLC), 209

About the Author

Robert Wolff, Ph.D., is a former editor of *Muscle & Fitness* and has worked with the world's biggest bodybuilding and fitness stars, including fitness legends Arnold Schwarzenegger and Evander Holyfield. Wolff is the author of numerous books including *Bodybuilding 101; Robert Wolff's Book of Great Workouts; Home Bodybuilding; The Knockout Workout with Mia St. John;* and *Dr. Robert Wolff's Great Body, Great Life Program.* He lives in New York City. For more information visit www.RobertWolff.com.

CPSIA information can be obtained at www.ICGtesting.com
Printed in the USA
LVOW11s1436290913

354600LV00007B/245/P

9 780071 635875